TWAYNE'S WORLD AUTHORS SERIES

A Survey of the World's Literature

CANADA

Joseph Jones, University of Texas

EDITOR

Ralph Gustafson

TWAS 531

RALPH GUSTAFSON

By WENDY KEITNER

University of Guelph

TWAYNE PUBLISHERS

A DIVISION OF G. K. HALL & CO., BOSTON

Published in 1979 by Twayne Publishers,
A Division of G. K. Hall & Co.

Printed on permanent/durable acid-free paper and bound
in the United States of America

First Printing

Keitner, Wendy, 1948–
Ralph Gustafson.

(Twayne's world authors series ; TWAS 531 : Canada)
Bibliography: pp. 164–66.
Includes index.
1. Gustafson, Ralph, 1909–
—Criticism and interpretation.
PR9199.3G8Z75   811'.5'2   78-20795
ISBN 0-8057-6373-2

For Gabor and Chimène

Contents

About the Author

Wendy Robbins Keitner, who is currently Assistant Professor of English at the University of Guelph, Ontario, Canada, was born in Saint Jean, Quebec, in 1948, and graduated from Bishop's University, Lennoxville (where she studied under Ralph Gustafson) with a B.A. Honors in English and French. At Queen's University, Kingston, Ontario, she completed an M.A. and a Ph.D.; her 1973 doctoral dissertation was entitled "Ralph Gustafson: Heir of Centuries in a Country without Myths."

On a world tour, she did bibliographic research in Commonwealth literature for Queen's University and the Canadian Association for Commonwealth Literature and Language Studies. In 1974, she joined the Department of English at the University of Guelph where she teaches courses in Canadian Literature, Women in Literature, and Major Modern Writers. In 1975, she introduced the university's first course in Commonwealth Literature.

Her publications include *Horizon: An Introduction to Canadian Literary Studies* and the chapter on "Canada" in *Commonwealth Literature: A Handbook of Select Reading Lists,* both of which were co-authored with R. T. Robertson. Her reviews and articles primarily on Canadian and Commonwealth writers have appeared in such journals as the *ACLALS Bulletin, Canadian Literature, Canadian Newsletter of Research on Women, Humanities Association Review, Quarry,* and *Sphinx.* She serves on the advisory board of *Atlantis* and is a contributing editor of the *Women's Studies Newsletter.* Recently, she co-guestedited a special issue of *World Literature Written in English* devoted to women writers of the Commonwealth.

Preface

When I first became interested in Ralph Gustafson's writing early in the 1970's, only two substantial studies of his work had been published—Louis Dudek's "Two Canadian Poets: Ralph Gustafson and Eli Mandel" and S. G. Mullins's "Ralph Gustafson's Poetry." Having appeared in *Culture* back in 1961, both were out of date. That Gustafson's work had been badly neglected by critics, scholars, and teachers of Canadian literature was readily demonstrable up to 1975. With the selection that year of *Fire on Stone*—his ninth significant book of poems—for the Governor General's Literary Award, the critical tide began to turn; several important Canadian literary journals published extended review articles or retrospective analyses, such as Robin Skelton's probing study "Ralph Gustafson: A Review and Retrospect" which appeared in *Mosaic*. Gustafson's almost simultaneous winning of the A. J. M. Smith Award for Poetry from Michigan State University spread interest in his work to a wider audience. Despite the recent spate of critical activity, however, a largely unbreached wall of ignorance, built of the fixed ideas that his writing is insurmountably erudite and too Eurocentric to have direct relevance for the average reader or student of Canadian literature, still shields Gustafson's work from a more popular reading.

This study, the first of its kind, is intended then primarily to promote the fuller and more adequate understanding of Gustafson's creative writing in both poetry and prose. Although he has earned international acclaim for his anthologies of Canadian literature and holds an established national position as a music critic with the Canadian Broadcasting Corporation, I chose not to include discussion of these aspects of his career. Given the relative obscurity, diversity, and rich complexity of Gustafson's literary *oeuvre*, I have instead devoted all my allotted space to exploring his poems, verse drama, and related short stories which present some of the same central themes.

The attempt to make Gustafson's creative work more accessible has been carried out in several ways. This study begins with a brief literary biography which traces Gustafson's development from his youth in Quebec, through the period of establishing of a writing career in England and the United States, to his maturity as professor of English and poet in residence at Bishop's University in Lennoxville, Quebec. Major literary influences, first British and later American, as well as key thematic concerns—such as the conflict between passion and intellect or between religion and art—thus are initially presented in direct relation to the writer's life and environment.

Chapter 2 outlines the chronological development of Gustafson's poetic style and suggests his position in relation to the tradition of Canadian poetry at large, showing how the pattern of his poetic growth depicts in miniature the general development of Canadian poetry from its beginnings in imitation of British models, through a period of modernization following the lead of key British and American writers, to a more vigorously independent maturity. Brief analyses of Gustafson's first books, including his verse drama *Alfred the Great*, are given here, while Chapter 3 offers fuller discussion of the more important and interesting works of his transitional period which are gathered together in the retrospective *Flight into Darkness* published in 1944.

Chapter 4 presents the first intensive study of Gustafson's prose fiction, concentrating on the stories collected in *The Brazen Tower* but referring also to uncollected stories and mentioning very briefly his one novel (unpublished) which, like most of the best stories, is set in the Quebec townships and probes the twin themes of love and repression. Crossreferences to poems are included frequently in order to point up important links between Gustafson's work in various genres and to underscore the constancy of his central insights concerning the supreme values of love and freedom to express love.

Chapters 5 and 6, which constitute the core of this study, give close readings with detailed annotation and interpretation of a comprehensive selection of individual poems from each of the eight books written in Gustafson's maturity, from *Rivers among Rocks* of 1960 to *Corners in the Glass* of 1977. In order to establish the validity of some of my interpretations of difficult or contentious material, I have supported my argument with references to manuscript drafts of the poems, documentation attached to them, and occasionally to correspondence with the author. In addition to providing this detailed study of separate poems, I have attempted to sketch in outline the general trends, developments, and new departures represented by each book of poetry as a whole, while noting throughout patterns of recurring themes and images. To give coherence and shape to this more abstract discussion, I have directed attention repeatedly to one structuring and basic conflict—that between time and space, history (largely European) and geography (Canadian), or, in terms more specific to Canadian criticism, between civilization and the wilderness.

While accentuating Gustafson's individuality in style, subject, and theme, I have endeavored simultaneously to relate his writing to the main body of Canadian literature in English; the conclusion of this study offers both an assessment of Gustafson's particular contribution and also an estimation of his ultimate place in this national tradition.

WENDY KEITNER

University of Guelph

Acknowledgments

I wish to acknowledge my gratitude to the many men and women who have been instrumental in helping me to research and write this book. My first expression of thanks must go to Ralph Gustafson himself for arranging the poetry readings by his fellow Canadian poets at Bishop's University in the mid 1960's which provided my initiation into Canadian literature; for allowing me access to unpublished material in his possession, including the typescript of "No Music in the Nightingale"; and for generous assistance through interviews, lengthy correspondence, and personally made corrections and suggestions particularly for the biographical section of this book.

For encouraging my study of Gustafson's work during my postgraduate years at Queen's University, I should like to express my lasting appreciation to my doctoral dissertation supervisor, Professor Douglas Spettigue, both for his careful scrutiny of my research and for the fine example he sets with his own. My thanks go also to Professor David Helwig for many fruitful suggestions made during the final stages of preparation of the dissertation; to Mr. Richard Giles, editor of the *Hopkins Quarterly* and my colleague at the University of Guelph, for numerous informal consultations about American and British sources and analogues; and to Ms Linda Sandler for allowing me to quote freely from the transcript of her probing interview with Gustafson in August 1975.

For facilitating my research among manuscript and rare materials, and for permission to quote, I should like to thank the librarians and archivists in charge of Gustafson papers at the Lockwood Memorial Library, State University of New York at Buffalo; the Murray Memorial Library, University of Saskatchewan at Saskatoon; and, above all, Queen's University Archives, Kingston, where the manuscripts of Gustafson's most important works—those dating from 1960 on—are housed.

For keeping my working bibliography of Gustafson's publications up to date, I should like to thank my research assistant, Ms Isabel

Acknowledgments

Guthrie, a student in Library Science at the University of Toronto, and also the late L. M. Allison, Librarian of the John Bassett Memorial Library, Bishop's University, Lennoxville, who began compilation of the first comprehensive Gustafson bibliography and allowed me to consult his work in progress in the early 1970's.

For financial assistance at various stages of my work, I thank the Canada Council, the Queen Elizabeth II Ontario Scholarship Committee, and both the Research Advisory Board and the Dean of the College of Arts, Professor Tom Settle, of the University of Guelph. For typing the penultimate draft of the book, my thanks to Ms Joanne Robinson, and for the final copy, to Ms Joan Barr. I owe a very special thanks as well to Ms Ratna Jeyabalan and Ms Barbara Miller whose loving care of my young daughter freed me to write this book, and above all to my husband, Gabor Keitner, M.D., for his selfless support of my career by making our marriage a genuine partnership.

In addition, I wish to acknowledge permission to quote from personal correspondence by Richard Arnell, Earle Birney, Northrop Frye, Ralph Gustafson, George Jonas, Yousuf Karsh, and A. J. M. Smith. For permission to reprint the following poems by Ralph Gustafson I also thank The Canadian Publishers, McClelland and Stewart Limited, Toronto: "The Courtyard" from *Sift in an Hour-glass*, "Old Lady Seen Briefly at Patras" and "Agamemnon's Mask: Archeological Museum, Athens" from *Ixion's Wheel*, "Hyacinths with Brevity" and "Bishop Erik Grave's Grave" from *Fire on Stone*, and "Wednesday at North Hatley" and "Poem in Late August" from *Corners in the Glass*.

Chronology

1942 *Anthology of Canadian Poetry (English)* brings international acclaim; publishes *Lyrics Unromantic.*

1943 Edits *A Little Anthology of Canadian Poets*; guest edits Canadian number of *Voices*; is anthologized by A. J. M. Smith in *Book of Canadian Poetry.*

1944 *Flight into Darkness*; Canadian Accent.

1945 *A Guide to Reading: Poetry and Canada*; becomes New York correspondent for *First Statement,* then regional editor for *Northern Review*; starts writing record liners.

1946 Anthologized by Selden Rodman in *New Anthology of Modern Poetry*; travels to Brazil.

1948 "The Human Fly" is anthologized by Martha Foley in *Best American Short Stories,* "The Thicket" by Edwin Seaver in *Cross-Section 1948*; edits Canadian section of Commonwealth number of *Voices.*

1949 "Summer Storm" is listed on Honor Roll of *Best American Short Stories.*

1950 "The Pigeon" is anthologized in *Best American Short Stories* and wins Short Fiction Prize from *Northern Review.*

1952 "The Pigeon" is anthologized by Desmond Pacey in *A Book of Canadian Stories.*

1952– Works on novel (unpublished), "No Music in the Nightingale:
1958 An Ironic Comedy."

1954 Premiere of ballet of "The Pigeon" at Miami University, Ohio.

1955 Delegate to Writers' Conference, Kingston, Ontario.

1957 Poems anthologized by F. R. Scott and A. J. M. Smith in *The Blasted Pine.*

1958 *Penguin Book of Canadian Verse*; marries Elisabeth Renninger.

1959 Awarded Senior Fellowship of the Canada Council; travels across Canada to the Yukon; elected to P.E.N. Club.

1960 *Rivers among Rocks*; Rocky Mountain Poems. Begins ongoing series of radio broadcasts of music criticism for Canadian BCroadcasting Corporation. "The Piegeon" anthologized by Robert Weaver in *Canadian Short Stories*; poems anthologized by A. J. M. Smith in *Oxford Book of Canadian Verse in English and French.*

1961 Wins Borestone Mountain Poetry Award for *Rocky Mountain Poems*; guest edits Canadian number of *Poetry Pilot: The Bulletin of the Academy of American Poets.*

1962 Travels to Britain, continental Europe, and Scandinavia;

poems anthologized by Irving Layton in *Love Where the Nights Are Long.*

1963   Upon being appointed to faculty of Department of English, Bishop's University, returns to Canada to reside in North Hatley; receives Master of Arts from Oxford; reads at Foster Poetry Conference in Quebec.

1965   Travels to Greece, Egypt, Italy, Turkey, and Western Europe; begins reports on Wagner at Bayreuth Festivals; poems anthologized by John Glassco in *English Poetry in Quebec* and by A. J. M. Smith in *Oxford Book of Canadian Verse.*

1966   *Sift in an Hourglass*; appointed poet in residence at Bishop's University; charter member of League of Canadian Poets; anthologized by Carl Klinck and R. E. Watters in *Canadian Anthology.*

1967   Publishes revised edition of *Penguin Book of Canadian Verse*; travels to Britain and Europe; anthologized by A. J. M. Smith in *Modern Canadian Verse in English and French*; gives poetry readings in Maritimes.

1968   Awarded Canada Council Grant to Artist.

1969   *Ixion's Wheel*; travels to Czechoslovakia and Hungary.

1970   Premiere of "Nocturne: Prague 1968," a mixed media presentation, at Bishop's University Centennial Theater, and subsequently at Hofstra University, New York. He is anthologized by John Robert Colombo in *How Do I Love Thee?*

1971   Receives Canada Council Senior Arts Award; travels to South Pacific and Japan, reading his work in Australia and Hawaii.

1972   *Selected Poems*; *Theme and Variations for Sounding Brass*; Canadian delegate to U. K. World Book Year, reading at several British universities.

1973   Doctorate of Literature, Honoris Causa, conferred by Mount Allison University.

1974   *Fire on Stone*; *The Brazen Tower*; taping of Gustafson Piano Library begun by Department of Music, Bishop's University.

1975   Wins Canadian Governor General's Literary Award and A. J. M. Smith Award for Poetry from Michigan State University for *Fire on Stone*; publishes second revised version of *Penguin Book of Canadian Verse*; reads in Massachusetts, Ontario, and at Conference on Canadian Literature at University of Leeds, England.

1976   Is named Canadian Department of External Affairs delegate (together with Al Purdy) to Russia; reading tour of Western Canada.

1977 *Corners in the Glass*; delegate to Symposium on Canadian Culture in Washington, D. C.; Library of Congress reading of his poems is taped; retires from teaching at Bishop's University; receives Queen's Silver Jubilee Medal.

1978 *Soviet Poems.*

CHAPTER 1

Biography

AS several recent critical studies have argued, one of the major themes of Canadian and Quebec literature from pioneer times to the present is the antagonism between civilization and the wilderness. The contest between forces of human tradition and desire and those of geography—a struggle, as many writers have envisioned it, between love and death—is a central motif in works stretching from Susanna Moodie through Ned Pratt to Al Purdy. It is also one of the most dominant themes in the writing of Ralph Gustafson.

In Gustafson's case, the tension created by the divergent pulls of culture (largely European) and nature (specifically Canadian) has interesting autobiographical sources, structures the pattern of his poetic development—which follows processes of colonization and decolonization in style, subject, and theme—and even dictates the course of his career. In broad outline, Gustafson's life divides into three distinct phases: formative years in Quebec (1909–30), middle years first in England (1930–39) then in the United States (1939–63), and later years combining residency in Quebec with world travel. Several important parallels between Gustafson's life and literary work, taken together with his personal statement that "living is prerequisite to the making of poems,"[1] suggest the need to begin this study by sketching a brief literary biography.

I Early Years: Eastern Townships of Quebec

The second child of a Canadian born mother and a Swedish immigrant father, Ralph Barker Gustafson was born on 16 August 1909—the same year as Abraham Klein, Dorothy Livesay, and Malcolm Lowry. His birthplace was the Quebec mining village of Lime Ridge where his maternal grandfather—who is sketched in the short story "The Circus"—held the influential position of superintendent of the Dominion Lime Company. Ralph Gustafson and his sister Pauline spent the formative years of childhood and adolescence in the neighboring city of Sherbrooke; the Eastern Townships of Quebec and even the family's wooden frame house on Wolfe (now Belvédère) Street provide the setting for several autobiographical stories about childhood and maturation.

The numerous cultural and personality differences between Ralph Gustafson's parents perhaps lie at the source of the deep divisions separating his international from his more regional commitments, and his aesthetic from his social interests. Gertrude Ella Barker Gustafson, his mother, was from an established Anglo-Quebec family descended from United Empire Loyalists. A cultured upper-class woman and a devoted member of Saint Peter's Anglican Church in Sherbrooke, Gertrude Gustafson passed on to her son a love of literature, art, and music—especially piano playing at which they both excelled. She taught her young son religion, took him to sing in the boys' church choir, and later tried to guide him towards a career in the Anglican ministry. While this early religious training left an indelible impression on him revealed in themes from both his poetry and prose fiction, Gustafson's overriding passion for the arts was evident well before he matriculated from Sherbrooke High School in 1926. During his high school years, Gustafson met the young Yousuf Karsh (who did his portrait more than twenty years later when both were residing in New York); Karsh remembers Gustafson in his youth as "always very sensitive and intellectual. There was no doubt that he would become a man of letters."[2] Still, so deep is his love of music that Gustafson confesses even now that he would almost prefer being a professional pianist to being a writer; his broadcasts of music criticism for the Canadian Broadcasting Corporation—continuing since 1960—have earned him a considerable reputation in this field, while over the years Gustafson and his wife together have collected a library of piano recordings so complete that the International Piano Library in New York occasionally asks them to supply material. This deep musical undercurrent perceptibly influences the verbal melody, rhythm, form, and even subject matter of Gustafson's writing.

While the guidance of his genteel mother was considerable (Gustafson's *Golden Chalice* is dedicated to "Her who first brought Beauty, My Mother"), the influence of his father, Carl Otto Gustafson—a volatile, independent, and equally artistic man—is important also. Carl Gustafson had set out for North America from Wexio, Sweden, at the end of the 1880's to join his adventurous older brother John who, having already crossed the Atlantic, was working as a dynamiter in the lime kilns of Lime Ridge. (Ralph Gustafson later recreated his Uncle John's immigrant experiences in Wolfe County in his unpublished regional novel, "No Music in the Nightingale: An Ironic Comedy.") Carl Gustafson first studied in New York then worked in Illinois as a movie cameraman before establishing himself as a photographer in Sherbrooke, Quebec. Although he seems not to have attained any great measure of financial security, especially during the depression years, he did achieve distinction: his artistic regional photographs—in somewhat the same vein as earlier Bartlett prints—are still exhibited in the Eastern Townships. Ralph Gustafson's Sherbrooke boyhood as a photographer's son supplies material for several of his short stories, while his eye for natural detail and his *wanderlust* apparently are the double-edged legacy of his father and paternal uncle.

At the age of seventeen, Ralph Gustafson entered Bishop's University where his literary studies were encouraged by minor Canadian poets Frank Oliver Call and Canon (later Archdeacon) Frederick George Scott. Still at this period Bishop's University was an institution predominantly for the training of Anglican clergy, which suggests again that the tension between religion and art which surfaces in Gustafson's writing—however classic a conflict—is distinctly autobiographical in character. But above all Gustafson was fired with the ambition to be another Keats (without consumption). That his literary apprenticeship was served to the writers of the outmoded British Romantic tradition is explained in part by the fact that courses in English literature at Bishop's in the 1920's did not extend beyond Swinburne. His undergraduate education did not expose him to Modernists such as Hopkins, Yeats, Pound, or Eliot; and although he was in contact with F. O. Call, a stylistic innovator and early Canadian advocate of free verse, Gustafson remained oblivious of the student-led literary rebellion being fomented a hundred miles away in Montreal at McGill University by Frank Scott and A. J. M. Smith. Independently he studied the history of Canadian literature, developing the special interest which would culminate in his series of anthologies of Canadian writing in the 1940's. But his own early poetry, mired in an outdated foreign tradition, does not belong to the first phase of the Canadian Modernist movement even though Gustafson was of the same student generation that gave it impetus and direction.

The year 1929 stands out in Gustafson's early career. It culminated in his graduating from university with a Bachelor of Arts degree in

Honors English and History, ranking first in his class and winning several distinctions, including prizes for a poem on music and an article on the history of Canadian literature since Confederation as well as the Governor General's Medal. It also marked the publication of his first short story, an Edgar Allan Poe thriller titled "The Last Experiment of Dr. Brugge," in the university's literary magazine the *Mitre*, and his first poems—"Snowfall" in *Willison's Monthly* and "Immutability" in the Canadian Authors' Association *Poetry Year Book*. The following year, while working as music master at nearby Bishop's College School, Gustafson completed a Master's degree in English at Bishop's University. His thesis, "The Sensuous Imagery of Shelley and Keats," underscores the considerable influence of the English Romantics on his early career.

As Gustafson matured, the isolation and provincialism of the townships and of Canada generally began to prey on him. In an interview in 1975 he reflected that "looking back on the community now, of course, it strikes me as village pump. It wasn't sophisticated—in other words it wasn't cosmopolitan. Sherbrooke's population at that time was only thirty or thirty-five thousand. . . . It was still country."[3] The rural quality of the community meant that life seemed close to nature, innocent, ideal; but people sharing a small-town mentality could also be narrowminded, ingrown, and philistine. The population of Sherbrooke and environs had sufficient cohesiveness for strong social pressure requiring conformity to restrictive conventions to be relentlessly exerted. Gustafson traces this pious, life-inhibiting morality mainly to the Methodist and Presbyterian churches. Although Anglican himself, his artistic sensibilities were frustrated by the general climate of repression in which pleasure was equated with sin, the arts were distrusted, and work leading to pragmatic success was esteemed as being of the highest value. His later poetry attacks certain Christian beliefs and practices, while his prose fiction typically portrays the dilemmas of sensitive and creative young people who are thwarted by an unsympathetic, puritanical environment. The theme of conflict between artist and society, one of the most pervasive in Canadian as well as older literatures, haunts Gustafson.

He explicitly sought escape from the parochial clutches of the townships in 1930 by leaving (with the aid of an I.O.D.E. scholarship) for Oxford then other cosmopolitan cities abroad, not to return to Canada except for brief interludes for more than thirty years. Like so many Canadian writers of his own generation and earlier, Gustafson has an intense love/hate relationship with his country. His writing in both prose and poetry reveals frustration with the puritanical and philistine Canadian mentality. Also running through his works, however, counterpointed against negative depictions of small-town society and attacks on the church, is the theme of profound and abiding love for the natural beauties of Canada, from the Yukon and the Rocky Mountains to the forested mountains and rolling hills, the quiet lakes and abundant rivers of the Eastern Townships of Quebec, and the quasireligious transcendence they evoke. Finally, later in life, Gustafson was to settle permanently in North Hatley on the shores of Lake Massawippi not many miles from his birthplace, in the same secluded artistic community frequented by other English Quebec poets such as Frank Scott, A. J. M. Smith, John Glassco, and Doug Jones. Gustafson ultimately recognizes that the townships is "a community and a geography which has profoundly affected all our poetry."[4]

II *Expatriate Years: England*

In 1930 Ralph Gustafson entered Keble College, Oxford, determined to become a poet in the tradition of "the Greats" of English literature. The typically colonial mentality thrown into prominence by this aspiration was matched by the imperiousness of an Oxford administration which required him, despite two Canadian university degrees, to register as a junior student in the Bachelor of Arts program. In new surroundings and several years older than fellow undergraduates from Britain, no doubt Gustafson was equally as ill at ease as the young Canadian expatriate who narrates "Surrey Harvest," one of his early short stories.

During three years of literary studies at Oxford, Gustafson published work twice in the annual *Oxford Poetry* and completed the manuscript of his first book of poetry, *The Golden Chalice*. His reading extended his knowledge of English literature and language back as far as the Anglo-Saxon period; the discovery of Old English poetry left an unmistakable influence on his verbal music and poetic vocabulary. Further, the historical information gathered about that period, combined with his wanderings around England, provided a base of fact and detail for his second book, the verse drama *Alfred the Great*.

Graduating from Oxford with a second Bachelor of Arts degree in 1933, Gustafson returned to Canada in the midst of the depression to the only teaching position he was able to procure—a poorly paid post at Saint Alban's School for Boys in Brockville, Ontario. Within a year he found that Southeastern Ontario was not much less parochial than the townships of Quebec. He deeply missed the intellectual and cultural life of England, and in 1934, the year of his mother's death, he returned to live in London where music, theater, and poetry flourished despite the threat of war. He supported himself by private tutoring, freelance journalism—which ranged from designing cross-word puzzles to writing articles for the *Spectator* and *Life and Letters*—and also by publishing poetry in *Cornhill* and *Poetry: A Magazine of Verse*. At this time as well, his first two books of verse were released by London publishing houses: in 1935 *The Golden Chalice*, a lushly Romantic volume begun during his township years (which nonetheless won the Prix David, a Quebec Government Literary Award), and in 1937 *Alfred the Great*.

Critics have suggested that W. H. Auden's adult career began with a rejection from T. S. Eliot; it can be argued with equal validity that Ralph Gustafson's adult career began with a rejection from Geoffrey Grigson. When poems Gustafson submitted to *New Verse* in 1932 were turned down by the influential editor as static and conventional, Gustafson—stung—immersed himself in the latest English poetry in an effort to overhaul his poetic style and bring himself up to date. Moving beyond his nineteenth-century models, during the mid 1930's he read and reread contemporary writers including Lawrence, Eliot, Yeats, Auden, Spender, and MacNeice. Later he was also to discover Pound and Stevens who, together with Browning, remain among his progenitors.

In England in the company of other expatriate artists, particularly the internationally renowned Canadian pianist Ellen Ballon and American sculptor Sally Ryan, Gustafson enjoyed social and cultural events on a scale unavailable to him in Canada. He had innumerable opportunities to listen to the greatest musicians then before the public, including Rosenthal, Hofmann, Cortot, Bauer, Paderewski, Moiseiwitsch, Schnable, Solomon, Beecham, Kreisler, and Elman. As the society news in *Mayfair* documents, Gustafson moved in prominent social circles. At one London tea in Ellen Ballon's honor, Gustafson was presented to the Prince of Wales; on another occasion he was the guest of President Roosevelt at a private White House concert given by Ballon. Yet with the outbreak of World War II, Gustafson decided to leave London for New York. He claims to have moved for the sake of music rather than for any political reasons in a relocation which may have been prompted by events in Ballon's career; Gustafson was closely connected with her from the 1930's until his late marriage to Elisabeth Renninger in 1958.[5]

III *Expatriate Years: U.S.A.*

In New York Gustafson began compilation of the paperback *Anthology of Canadian Poetry (English)*, commissioned by Allan Lane of Penguin Books whose acquaintance he had made in London. The book was intended initially for distribution to Canadian soldiers abroad during the war, but the assignment of the anthology did not noticeably influence Gustafson's selections. He was motivated to undertake a major revaluation of Canadian poetry because of vexation with the indifference of anthologists of world literature in English towards Canadian writing and because he recognized that collections of Canadian literature circulating in Canada itself (such as Wilfred Campbell's 1913 *Oxford Book of Canadian Verse* or John Garvin's 1916 *Canadian Poets*) were undiscriminating and out of date.

During the selection process, Gustafson ran into countless bureaucratic difficulties and delays. For a start, publishers who held copyright to individual titles by Canadian poets and to existing anthologies were highly suspicious of the new paperback market. Gustafson's voluminous correspondence with poets and publishers during this period reveals his remarkable candor, humility, and fortitude. His dedication to the cause of Canadian literature is also indicated by the fact that in the end he assumed a personal debt of over a thousand dollars in order to clear copyrights. Published in 1942, Gustafson's original Penguin anthology represents his single most important critical contribution to the development of Canadian literature. More than two decades before cultural nationalism became a popular issue in Canada, this pioneering collection demonstrated to an international audience that there was indeed a vital and up-to-date tradition of Canadian poetry whose substantial dimensions it displayed. The sale around the world of fifty thousand copies of *Anthology of Canadian Poetry (English)* gave Gustafson the satisfaction of knowing, as he wrote to Robert Finch in 1946, that Canadian poetry was "no longer an intramural affair."[6]

His second anthology (unpublished) was a joint venture with A. J. M. Smith. Correspondence reveals that Gustafson and Smith in the early 1940's were working on an anthology of contemporary work tentatively entitled "Canadian Poetry Today." Ultimately Smith seems to have incorporated at least part of it into his *Book of Canadian Poetry*,[7] while the success of Gustafson's Penguin anthology led him to other independent editorial ventures: guest editing a special Canadian issue of *Voices* and gathering for New Direction's Poets of the Year Series a short collection of contemporary Canadian poetry—his *Little Anthology of Canadian Poets*—both published in 1943. Another anthology for Penguin Books followed; devoted primarily to prose, it was intended to be a continuing project similar to *New Writing*, the English quarterly which Penguin published through the 1940's (in fact the project was tentatively entitled "New Writing Canada"). In 1944 the first volume, *Canadian Accent: A Collection of Stories and Poems by Contemporary Writers from Canada*, was published. Although this book sold well abroad, it was virtually unavailable in Canada since Gustafson could not persuade any Canadian publisher to present it. "Canadian Accent II," a sequel, was assembled. It included the work of such then little known writers as Raymond Knister, Irving Layton, Earle Birney, and Emily Carr; but this volume was delayed and finally abandoned because of the wartime restriction on paper and a recession in the publishing industry. Gustafson salvaged only the preface, publishing it in 1949 as "Writing and Canada" in *Life and Letters and the London Mercury*.

While Gustafson was establishing a reputation in Canadian literature in this way, ironically enough he was residing in the United States and employed by the British government. From 1942 to 1946 he did daily surveys of American newspapers and radio for the British Information Services, cabling a synopsis to London each night for the cabinet meeting next morning. One digest he did at the time the Russians were agitating for a second front received the personal compliments of Churchill. After the end of the war, Gustafson was invited to stay on as head of the survey department, but he decided to leave so that he could devote himself to his own writing.

In addition to this demanding survey work and his anthologizing of Canadian literature, in the early 1940's Gustafson produced four books of his own poetry: *Poems (1940), Epithalamium in Time of War, Lyrics Unromantic,* and *Flight into Darkness*. The offprinted sequence of poems from the *Sewanee Review* published as *Poems (1940)*, along with *Epithalamium in Time of War*, which was composed for the 1941 marriage of his sister, and *Lyrics Unromantic* of 1942 (both privately printed in New York), clearly are works in transition. The title of the latter collection indicates Gustafson's overt repudiation of his early mentors and Romantic attitude, but the modernization of his style was not instantaneous. Only *Flight into Darkness* of 1944 shows substantial evidence of his integration of the Modernist mode.

Gustafson's ties to the Canadian literary scene ostensibly were made more direct in 1945 when John Sutherland invited him to act as New York correspondent for the Montreal based periodical *First Statement*. When this little magazine merged with its rival *Preview* to become *Northern Review* later this same year, Gustafson's services were retained. He contributed a series of New York letters before resigning in 1947 over Sutherland's vitriolic attack on Robert Finch. Gustafson's personal efforts in financing, soliciting for, and distributing *Northern Review* and another new Canadian periodical *Here and Now* were unremitting, while his reviews of Canadian poetry for American journals continued for many years. Yet despite early personal ties with Sutherland and appearances in *First Statement* and *Northern Review* under his editorship, Gustafson never considered himself a part of the *First Statement* group. He knew the *Preview* poets somewhat better, meeting A. J. M. Smith through Leon Edel who was living in New York and, through early friendship with F. R. Scott, the others—Anderson, Klein, Page. But although Gustafson's educational background and modernized poetic style tended, like theirs, to be cosmopolitan and rather intellectual, he never felt a part of the *Preview* coterie either. Gustafson has always remained a loner, not belonging to any incorporated literary group.

By the mid 1940's, he began to channel his creative efforts into prose fiction. One of the reasons for this shift was economic: prose paid better, and financial considerations became more important after Gustafson left the employ of the British Information Services. He earned money by writing record liners and musical monographs as well as short stories. But regardless of motivation, Gustafson achieved distinction in the genre of the short story. Revealing a postwar consciousness of violence and psychological trauma, his fiction was published by such prestigious journals as *Atlantic Monthly, Story, Canadian Forum*, and *Queen's Quarterly*, and anthologized in Martha Foley's *Best American Short Stories* and Edwin Seaver's *Cross-Section*. His most celebrated story, "The Pigeon," not only won a fiction prize from *Northern Review* and appeared in the Foley anthology, but also was set to music for modern dance by Ronald Herder and given its ballet premiere at

Miami University, Ohio, in 1954 under the direction of Winford C. Cummings.[8]

Several times Gustafson tried to interest publishers in a collection of his stories, but they always urged him to write a novel first. Obligingly, he began to work in the mid 1950's on "No Music in the Nightingale: An Ironic Comedy," which he set in the Eastern Townships in the fictional village of Lime Rock. Patterned on members of Gustafson's own family, the main characters are the daughter of the owner of the lime kiln, Ann Bradshaw; a Scandinavian immigrant's son, Johnny Gulbranson, who works in the pits and dreams of becoming a photographer; and the poetic Brand Dorset. Like so many of his stories, this regional novel explores the moral character of the townships, or more particularly Wolfe County, with its intimacies, conventions, and hostility to artists. The novel was never published, but a collection of Gustafson's stories appeared belatedly in 1974 as *The Brazen Tower*. The limited edition of this hand-set book, designed and printed by George McDonagh at his Roger Ascham Press in Tillsonburg, Ontario, sold out almost at once.

In the 1950's, too, Gustafson was urged to undertake an expansion of his first anthology. Preparation of a new *Penguin Book of Canadian Verse* necessitated an exhaustive rereading of two centuries of Canadian poetry and painstaking correspondence to clear permissions. A large number of now heavily anthologized Canadian poems were first given emphasis in Gustafson's collections; indeed Gustafson's preeminence as an anthologist is confirmed by the fact that this title, first published in 1958, is still in print, revised editions having been published in 1967 and 1975—despite an enormous proliferation of competing Canadian anthologies in the intervening years.

After more than a decade of editing anthologies and writing prose fiction, Gustafson redirected his energies to poetry in the late 1950's partly as a result of contacts with e. e. cummings, Auden, Spender, and William Carlos Williams; but unquestionably the chief catalyst was Elisabeth (Betty) Renninger, a warm and vivacious woman from Pennsylvania who had come to work as a nurse in New York and who shared Gustafson's passion for music. Many of the finest love poems of his career, including "Beach with White Cloud" and "Armorial," are written in the period just prior to 1958, the year of their marriage. The Gustafsons' honeymoon, spent in the Quebec townships, was followed by coast to coast travel across Canada, Ralph Gustafson being assisted financially by a Canada Council Senior Fellowship.

His sequence of poems on the Rockies and Canadian Northwest—
Rocky Mountain Poems—published in Vancouver in 1960 by
William McConnell at his Klanak Press, won the Borestone Mountain Poetry Award. Meanwhile in Toronto, McClelland and Stewart
brought out a very handsome edition of *Rivers among Rocks*,
collecting Gustafson's poetic output for the entire period 1944–59.

IV *Later Years: Regionalist and Internationalist*

In 1963 Gustafson was appointed to the Department of English at
his *alma mater*, Bishop's University, and once again took up Eastern
Townships residence. He belatedly paid the requisite fee to Oxford
and received in return his second Master of Arts degree. With the
responsibility of marriage, he was ready to give up the uncertain life
of freelance writing (although from 1960 to the present he has
continued to write music criticism at regular intervals); furthermore,
he had always intended to return to Canada one day. With the
wisdom of hindsight, he now wishes he had not stayed away so long,
attributing primarily to his absence the long neglect of his writing in
this country.

Gustafson taught courses in modern English, American, and
Canadian literature—a course he introduced into the curriculum—
from 1963 until his retirement in 1977. His life presently alternates
between quiet residence in North Hatley and extensive travel to many
parts of the world, including Europe, the Middle and Far East, the
South Pacific, and most recently the Soviet Union where he and Al
Purdy were State guests on an invited reading tour. This combination
of residency in the townships with world travel has made Gustafson's
later poems international in outlook, although paradoxically with
increasing intensity they also celebrate local beauty. Gustafson
recently described himself as "a sophisticated native; or a natural
cosmopolite; an extra-mural Canadian; a Canadian international; a
non-frontier loving Janus of great palaver."[9] Acceptance of such
dichotomies and apparent contradictions places Gustafson amongst
those other Canadian writers whom anthologist Malcolm Ross once
described as "thoroughgoing provincials (with a feeling for place),
and thoroughgoing citizens of the world (with a feeling for time)."[10]

Critics have suggested that Gustafson has been growing stylistically younger over the years, the modern part of his sensibility
coming to dominate the traditional part with increasing sureness. It is
equally apparent that he has been growing more distinctively Cana-

dian in subject matter. He has also become prolific, publishing between 1966 and 1977 six books of poems: *Sift in an Hourglass* (1966), *Ixion's Wheel* (1969), *Theme and Variations for Sounding Brass* (1972), *Selected Poems* (1972), *Fire on Stone* (1974), and *Corners in the Glass* (1977).[11] This prolificity during the years subsequent to Gustafson's marriage led A. J. M. Smith to suggest in a playful poem occasioned by Gustafson's being named poet in residence at Bishop's University in 1966 that Gustafson's *ars poetica* can be summed up in two small words: "my love." Gustafson uses just one: "Betty."

The poetry of Gustafson's maturity, typified by *Sift in an Hourglass* or *Ixion's Wheel* for example, illustrates the Yeatsian dictum that sex and death are the only subjects that can interest a serious mind. He focusses on the twin facts of love and life's brevity, regaling on this physical and imperfect world in spite, or rather the more urgently because, of a passionately held conviction that all things are doomed by time. The eternal theme of mutability here is unrelieved by faith in any ultimate justification. In 1966 the death of Gustafson's father (a death movingly retold in his finest short story, "The Tangles of Neaera's Hair") and in the winter of 1973 his own serious illness stemming from a pancreatic abscess underscored in personal terms this central theme of the brevity of existence. Always in his mature poems is to be found the paradox that awareness of love is simultaneously awareness of ephemerality.

The witness literature of *Theme and Variations for Sounding Brass* of 1972 stands apart in the Gustafson canon as the product of a deliberate decision to deal directly with the political brutalities of the times. The best known of these protest poems is "Nocturne: Prague 1968," which was given multi-media presentation at universities in Canada and the United States as well as being broadcast by the Canadian Broadcasting Corporation. *Selected Poems,* published in the same year, is a comprehensive presentation of the scope and depth of Gustafson's art over three decades, from the time of the transitional *Flight into Darkness* through *Ixion's Wheel.* It was followed by *Fire on Stone,* winner of the A. J. M. Smith Award for Poetry given by the Canadian-American Studies program at Michigan State University, and also the Governor General's Literary Award for 1974. This volume, together with *Corners in the Glass,* represents a rounding out of Gustafson's philosophical values and a major step towards the clarification of his style and the repatriation of his vision. But while these latest poems are far removed from his early idealistic Romanticism, his subjective mode and celebration of natural beauty underscore a basic and unwavering conviction that the transcendent is attainable only through affirmation of the sensuous universe.

In searching for values relevant to contemporary civilization, Gustafson sifts through history, too, not only geography. In the final analysis he shows himself to be (combining Michael Hornyansky's words with his own) "the heir of civilized centuries" in "a country without myths." Even during a literary era when themes of dissolution, exile, and alienation are rife, Gustafson's art issues ultimately in a rare sacrament of praise as he reaffirms the ageless values of life, love, sex, art, and freedom. What is hideous in life he sees but vaults above to rejoice in vital moments of beauty and happiness, and to celebrate human creativity, passion, and love. Although in his work the great antinomies—love and death, his symbolic fire and stone—remain irreconcilable, Gustafson's vision has a double hook which hauls in both the glory and the darkness.[12]

CHAPTER 2

Poetry of the 1930's: Derivation from Tradition

IN the introduction to his *Penguin Book of Canadian Verse*, Ralph Gustafson gives a short survey of the development of the Canadian poetic tradition, observing that "Canadian poetry came to maturity slowly and with difficulty."[1] The same generalization applies to the progression of his own poetic development, for it recapitulates in brief the general pattern of the growth of Canadian literature. Gustafson's anthology divides Canadian poetry from preConfederation times to the present into three main periods: (1) imitative infancy, beginning with the Shakespearean blank verse dramas of Heavysege, the Spenserian stanzas of Sangster, and the Wordsworthian or Keatsian nature lyrics written by the poets of Confederation; (2) transition, commencing in the 1920's with the poetry and militant criticism of A. J. M. Smith and Frank Scott who championed newer but still alien models—Yeats, Eliot, and the Imagists; (3) maturity, dating from the 1940's and the work of Earle Birney and Irving Layton, a period of vigorous and individualistic achievement.

Gustafson's own poetic development over the fifty years spanned by his writing career divides roughly into these same three periods. His poetry begins around 1930 in an initial phase of derivative Romanticism; around 1940 it passes through a transitional phase of modernization influenced by the work of Eliot, Hopkins, and the Auden-Spender-MacNeice group; and by 1960 it culminates in a distinctive, multifaceted maturity.

Processes of colonization and decolonization can be traced in Gustafson's work, as in that of many other Canadian and Commonwealth writers, for at first he aligned himself uncritically and to a very marked degree with British tradition. The initial period in his career as a poet (roughly covering the decade 1927–37) is characterized by a colonial-minded imitation of earlier English masters, primarily

Shakespeare, Keats, and Shelley. The diction of Gustafson's blank verse drama *Alfred the Great*, for example, contains innumerable Shakespearean echoes and allusions, while *The Golden Chalice*—taking its title from Gustafson's one long narrative poem written in Spenserian stanzas—is decorated opulently with Keatsian imagery. Gustafson's infatuation with the English Romantics is manifested, in fact, through the style of virtually all his work published prior to 1940. It is apparent, too, in the thematic orientation of a number of early poems such as "Vision," "Identity," and "Explanation" which celebrate the young poet's love which "with truth and beauty's one."[2]

His 1930 Master's thesis titled "The Sensous Imagery of Shelley and Keats" provides still further evidence of his worship of the Romantics. Gustafson writes of Keats that "his life-long devotion to the 'Principle of beauty in all things,' his dreamy solitude, his separation from dated soon-forgotten occurrences, theoretical philosophies, and localities, is perhaps the nearest parallel in English literature to the ideal existence which we all visualize for a poet. . . . He himself was a 'true poem'—beauteous, vital, passionate, and sincere."[3] Gustafson now makes light of his early longing to be another Keats, dismissing his first book of poetry as a horror of derivation; but well into the 1930's his writing evolved under the hypnotic influence of Keats's style and reveals a full acceptance of the Romantic aesthetic which equates beauty with truth.

I   The Golden Chalice

Gustafson's first book of verse, *The Golden Chalice* (1935), is juvenilia. In this overwritten, imitative collection of thirty-nine sonnets, one extended Spenserian narrative, and eleven other poems in various forms, the main theme is the afflatus of the young poet-lover. The egocentricity and inflated rhetoric of the poems are overwhelming; from the epigraph. Gustafson projects the poet as a quasidivinity with his

> Keen mind supremely conscious of a rash
> Immortal power to quaff with single breath
> The pungent wine of love and life, then dash
> The crystal goblet in the face of death. (9)

Dedicating himself to a life of sensations and their transmutation into art, Gustafson repeatedly presents himself in exaggerated Romantic postures at this stage in his development.

Flame and fire metaphors convey the urgency of the persona's passion, turning *The Golden Chalice* into a conflagration of images. Beauty consistently elicits a white hot response. The poet's words are intended to "strike mad fire"; his lover's nerves are frayed to "streaks of ragged fire"; a night "flame[s] sublime"; a sunset seems to be composed of "white-hot splinters"; even a rainbow set in the "dripping heavens" can appear to his imagination as "sun-burnt." Further lack of judgment and restraint is seen in Gustafson's use of synaesthesia. In an attempt to emulate Keats's luxuriant sensuousness, he relies on the technique of mixing sense impressions, often without proper regard for their cumulative effect. For instance, describing the effect of a young suitor's words on the lady he loves, Gustafson writes:

> Like music coloured with the heavy scent
> Of evening flowers, his words with vibrant stress
> Unloosed within her heart rich ravishment;
> As honey drugs the bee with lusciousness,
> Her senses stifled with such aching bliss. (40)

What is distressing about these particular lines is not only their bizarre amalgam of references and appeals to the various senses, however, but curiously enough, at the same time, their abstract quality which is indicated by such words as "ravishment," "lusciousness," and "bliss."

Poem titles themselves epitomize this tendency to abstract—"Constancy," "Explanation," "Consummation"—a defect especially noticeable in the suite of twenty sonnets opening *The Golden Chalice*. These sonnets center on the theme of young love and concern a stunningly beautiful young woman pianist from whom the persona has been separated by family intervention and physical distance. Despite the passion, frenzy, and angry frustration inspiring the poetry, it remains strangely abstract and impersonal; the loved one remains a vague, rhetorical presence, a series of apostrophes—"O Sweet," "O lovely lady."

The title poem attempts to present the theme of frustrated young love in a more dramatic and concrete way. This fifty-nine stanza narrative takes its inspiration from Boccaccio's *Decameron* where Fiametta initiates discourse on the theme of disastrously concluded love. The tale involves Tancred, Prince of Salerno, who causes his daughter's lover Guiscard to be slain, sending her his severed heart in a golden cup; the bereaved Ghismond fills this chalice with poison, drinks it, and, to Tancred's bitter regret, dies.

Gustafson remains faithful to the original plot, although he compresses the story-line by ignoring Ghismond's brief first marriage and subsequent widowhood and omitting the extended medieval discourse on fleshly appetite and the vagaries of Fortune which Boccaccio assigns his heroine to speak on her deathbed. Yet in subtle ways Gustafson transforms Ghismond from the sophisticated, experienced, determined, and rational woman of the *Decameron* into a more naive, dreamy, and passive virgin just awakening to her body's sexual urges and awareness of her father's jealous and possessive love. The chief innovation in Gustafson's version, however, is his sensuous depiction of the sumptuous Mediterranean setting. His use of Spenserian stanzas stalls the narrative, but it does allow for a leisurely survey of the opulent and exotic scene he creates. Gustafson depicts Tancred's palace as hung with Tharsian tapestries, smoking censers, and "Jewelled beds of many-pillowed ease" (35). Ghismond expires "While coloured casements splashed unnoticed strips/ Of crimson beauty down her drowsy clothes"; at her death, "Upon the tired softness of the bed/ Her lovely body lay: her careless hair/ Like some brown shadow on white snow outspread" (53). The mixing of sense impressions ("tired softness"), the studied misplacing of epithets ("drowsy clothes"), as well as the texture of the language and even the words themselves ("casements," "ease") are imitative of Keats and Shelley, of course; but inversion for the sake of rhyme notwithstanding, the poetry here—as in Al Purdy's first book, *The Enchanted Echo*—is skillful even if unforgiveably anachronistic.

Following the title poem are nineteen additional sonnets in which the imagery tends to be less vague and dreamy, and nine slightly more original poems, such as the two "songs" and one "nocturne" which mark Gustafson's earliest attempts to close the formal gap between poetry and music. A few poems deal with poetry itself, shrilly condemning the Modernist movement. The sonnet "To Those Concerned" indicts "Those modern poem-mongers, new, inane" who "splutter phrases reasonlessly sane/ On intricate obscurities" (61). "A Poet in Exile" is a lengthier critique of this "age of grovelling cynicism" (73) in which poets are "dismally inclined/ To uncourageous effort, swift despair" (77). While almost unreadably strident, this poem is an extended early statement of a theme which becomes increasingly important in Gustafson's poetry and prose fiction: the theme of *creator castratus*—the creative individual trapped in a stultifying environment. It also indirectly prophesies the strikingly affirmative attitude of most of his later work.

Other poems such as "Written in Kenilworth Castle," "At Hamlet's Grave, Elsinore," and "In Iffley Churchyard" provide the first examples of Gustafson's preoccupation with the profound yet common "lesson of rotting flesh" (57). "In Iffley Churchyard," which suggests a tension between two repositories of beauty—art ("tombstones") and nature ("sunlight," "blackbirds")—is the finest of these early graveside meditations. At its conclusion, the persona notices:

> Here at my feet the usual symbol crawls,
> A worm concludes the problem sages thresh—
> Of paltry use, when beauty thus slips between:
> The sunlight burns; from the eaves a blackbird calls. (57)

While many of these poems were composed during the course of travels to various historical monuments and famous ruins in Britain, continental Europe, and Scandinavia, a few spring from the rural Canadian scene. The best of these native poems, in which the style is noticeably less derivative and more vividly concrete, is "Winter Scene":

> Between long silences the river-ice
> Suddenly cracks and moves with winter's might;
> And from a lonely farm-house seen afar,
> A lazy smoke uncurls across the night. (67)

Gustafson's characteristic alternations between foreign and local concerns or between history and geography, his two poetic voices, and his major themes—love, death, the entrapment of the creative individual, and the beauty of nature—thus are already discernible in this first collection.

II   Alfred the Great

Set in ninth-century England and focussing on the interrelated themes of war, peace, love, and the safeguarding of Western civilization, Gustafson's second published book—*Alfred the Great*—was written in the mid 1930's as Europe slid irrecoverably towards World War II. This history play is not merely an escape into the romantic past. In it Gustafson makes an attempt to parallel the political drama of ninth-century England with the contemporary situation as Britain and her allies saw their peace treaties betrayed by Hitler and Mussolini.

With remarkable fidelity to historical fact as recorded in the *Anglo-Saxon Chronicle* and Asser's *Life of King Alfred*, Gustafson's three-act play traces the truces and battles of the Saxons under Alfred and the Danes under Guthrum around the period of the Treaty of Wedmore. The play opens in Wessex in December 877. Successive wars have already reduced Alfred's kingdom to one-third its former size; as the play begins, Alfred and his warriors return to Uffington Castle from yet another defeat, this time at Wantage. While the men drink mead in the hall, Alfred rallies them with praise, calling them men "whose strength can match defeat/Set off its lustre in the foil of loss."[4] Alfred embodies similar resilience himself, but he is troubled by the terms of this new defeat which have been accepted by Bishop Werwulf without proper consultation: Ethelred, the Saxon's strongest earl, has been left as hostage in the Danes' camp to be ransomed with Elfwyn, a beautiful young woman who was taken into Alfred's personal custody after the death in an earlier battle of her loyal father. In return for Elfwyn, Guthrum promises to leave Wessex in peace.

The Saxons are split in their reaction to Guthrum's pledge: Werferth, bishop of Worcester—a Chamberlain-like naif—urges appeasement; but Odda, aldorman of Devonshire, has no faith in treaties with the wily Danes. Alfred summarily rejects the exchange of Elfwyn for Ethelred, refusing to treat her as mere chattel, and concludes: "Our hope is war if we wish Wessex peace" (23). Fundamentally, however, Alfred hates the destructiveness and waste of war. His personal tenderness and great respect for learning (which, he believes, can be extended to his illiterate people only when peace flourishes) are qualities brought out by exchanges with his wife Elswitha, his ward Elfwyn, and his teacher, the hermit Plegmund. The long opening scene ends as Elfwyn courageously decides to go to the Danes' camp without Alfred's knowledge to secure the release of Ethelred, without whom her country's doom seems sealed.

Act 1 scene 2 shifts to the rowdy, pagan, Danish camp in the monastery church at Wantage, which Guthrum's men have ransacked and desecrated. They further demonstrate their scorn for Christianity by laying plans to attack Alfred at Chippenham while he celebrates Christmas, thereby also defying their pledge of peace. When Guthrum discovers that Elfwyn's submission to his terms is voluntary, and therefore presumably not binding on Alfred, he is infuriated and offers her as the prize in a lewd, beer drinking competition. She is spared this humiliation by Sigurd, young king of Zeeland; having fallen in love with her at first sight, he makes payment of her weight in gold. Next Bishop Werwulf comes to the Danes' camp with an offer from Alfred to buy back Elfwyn's freedom. The Danes kill him in cold blood, violating the code which protected an earl in open hall and further underscoring their treacherous nature. Act 1 then winds to a close with a lyrical exchange between the young lovers Elfwyn and Sigurd.

Act 2 takes place three months later. Having lost heavily at Chippenham, Alfred and a small band are living in exile in a rough, uncomfortable fort at Athelney, reduced to raiding the Danish camp for food. But Alfred remains kinglike and unconquerable in spirit, determined to make one final attempt to rescue Elfwyn and save Wessex. Before scene 1 ends, the aldormen Odda and Ethelhelm and the warrior Ingulf bring news that the tide of the Saxon fortunes has begun to turn with successes at Swanage and Cynwit Fort, the destruction of the Danish fleet, and the raising of a large force by Ethelred and Werferth who by now has abandoned his pacifist philosophy.

Scene 2 presents the Saxons at the zenith of their power, celebrating the victory of Wedmore. The defeated Danes have agreed to withdraw from Wessex and Mercia and to keep peace; they have even submitted to Christian baptism (except for Sigurd who refuses to play the hypocrite). Elfwyn is restored to the Saxons, and Sigurd in his turn is hostaged to guarantee the terms of the peace. This enables the lovers to continue to meet, even though it jeopardizes Sigurd's life—for Guthrum is already plotting to break his oath.

Act 3 takes place in Swanage three weeks later. The Saxons are at work building up their fleet when a messenger rushes into Alfred's palace with the news that the Danes have broken the truce and are massing at Rochester where their ally Hasten is positioned with three hundred ships from Frankland. The Saxons instantly attack and kill Sigurd. Coming upon the bloody scene, Alfred shows pity for the clumsy fate of the young king; respecting Sigurd's pagan beliefs, he gives his remains a sea burial. Elfwyn, dazed by the swiftness of the tragic event, wanders distractedly to the seaside, leaving Alfred to speculate on her secret love and to regret the rough denials of war. The play ends with Alfred's expression of paternal concern that "The brunt of all this tangled hate and war/Is hers" (110) and his lamentation that the time is still not ripe for the cherished pursuits of peace.

But resolute to the end in his conviction about the necessity to fight for peace, Alfred prepares once more to wage war against the enemy.

The core historical events of *Alfred the Great*—including the Danish attack on Chippenham, Alfred's retreat to the fen-fastness at Athelney, the Saxon victory at Edington, and the baptism of the Danes at Aller—are all authentic. Events peripheral to the main action but referred to during the course of the drama—such as the battles of Ashdown and Wareham, Halfdene's successes in Northumbria, the death of King Edmund, the Danish massing of ships in Frankland, and the breaking of the Peace of Wedmore by the Viking attack at Rochester—are also accurate, although the *Anglo-Saxon Chronicle* places the breaking of the peace some six years, not a scant three weeks, after its taking effect. Poetic licence allows for time compression and also imaginative reconstructions; for instance, the opening battle of Wantage is fictitious, although the Danish strategy of false retreat mentioned here is recorded by Asser in his account of a different Saxon defeat at Wilton in 871—the defeat in which Gustafson's fictitious Elfwyn lost her father.

What is most interesting about Gustafson's handling of his historical material is the way in which it can be seen as relevant to the European scene of the 1930's. The failure of the League of Nations in meeting the open defiance of the Treaty of Versailles with more than ineffectual verbal protests following Japan's invasion of Manchuria and of China proper in 1933, Italy's incursion into Abyssinia, and Germany's rearmament and occupation of the Rhineland in 1935 may be compared with the Vikings' systematic breaking of oaths in ninth-century England. In certain ways, Gustafson's play is even prophetic. The policy of appeasement pursued by France and Britain at Munich in 1938, the year after the publication of *Alfred the Great,* is similar to the position presented to Alfred by Werwulf; so too the selling-out of Poland resembles the Saxons' and Danes' bartering for peace with Elfwyn, a person over whom in any case they had no legitimate right to ownership or disposal. More specifically, Guthrum may be viewed in certain respects as an analogon for Hitler. Hitler's defiance of the Treaty of Versailles, followed by his cancellation of the non-aggression pact with Poland in 1939, resembles the Danish leader's successive breaches of faith after Wareham, Exeter, and Wedmore. The shortsighted majority of Saxons who "fear immediate issue/ More than future worse through present action" (60) find their twentieth-century counterparts in the supporters of Chamberlain with his infamous, bitterly ironic, post Munich pledge "I believe this is peace for our time." Gustafson's Alfred, sustaining the opposite position, is not unaware of the paradoxical nature of his platform—trying to win peace through war. Nevertheless, were Gustafson to have extended his play to include the outcome of the deciding battle of Rochester, it would have been seen that Alfred's side, like Churchill's, eventually triumphs.

Not only the progress of military events but also Gustafson's characterization of Alfred is essentially faithful to recorded fact. His portrayal of Alfred as the valiant military defender of a threatened Christendom and equally as a tender, sensitive man who has no love for war but much prefers learning, religion, and the pursuits of peace corresponds to portraits in the only contemporary biography extant and to Alfred's own prefaces. Like Asser's Alfred, Gustafson's titular hero is profoundly convinced of the values of Christianity and learning both for himself and his people. (One recalls that Milton, when searching for an epic subject from British history, as he records in *The Reason of Church Government,* found himself attracted by the concept of Alfred as a Christian hero.) While historically authentic, Gustafson's characterization of Alfred still allows him scope for introducing one of his own central themes: the fundamental antagonism between the temper of the times and cultivation of the arts. Alfred's final lament at the news of Sigurd's murder is not only for the inevitable postponement of the arts of peace—farming, poetry, and prayer—but also for thwarted love. He is sorry for "Such love, cramped by the hateful use of war,/Its rough denial" (110).

Although many of Gustafson's characters, even the minor ones, are mentioned by his historical sources—Halfdene, Ingwar, Hubba, Odda, Ethelred, Ethelred Mucill, and King Edmund—two major characters, the lovers Sigurd and Elfwyn, are fictitious. This would seem to indicate that Gustafson's originality lies not in his rendering of the war motif, but rather in his treatment once again of the theme of young love which ends tragically. The dramatization of the love between Sigurd and Elfwyn, moreover, represents a significant advance in terms of concreteness of treatment and competence with verse-dialogue over Gustafson's narrative poem "The Golden Chalice." A comparison of the speeches of the earlier lover Guiscard with Sigurd's in *Alfred the Great* demonstrates Gustafson's increasing poetic subtlety. When Guiscard kisses his lover for the first time, he murmurs the rather abstract statement: "My soul's delight,/I feared in these black caverns sudden harms/Might fall—but thy sweet lips dispel all dread alarms" (45). The dialogue between Sigurd and Elfwyn generally is more convincing and the speech rhythms more supple. At one point Sigurd tells Elfwyn:

> The soft of you—at dawn,
> When you came through the gate—it was not light
> Enough for me to see how frost had silvered it.
> One moment in the half-dark you were in
> My arms—till you regained your pace. You have
> Forgot. But I—the pressure of your body
> Urged this madness to extreme—from noon
> Within the cloister I cursed myself a fool;
> You came, walking within the close. I knew
> This rugged Sigurd, more solemn on a flint
> Within his horse's shoe than on the sum
> Of womankind, was then a hopeless beggar
> After love—I had but to note the way
> Your cloak drew close about your shoulder—
> The sudden naked rhythm of your hair,
> As careless of the cold you loosed the hood
> Against the sun—the gentle depth of hurt
> Within your eyes—it struck along my pulse
> As though a fist had smashed my forward mouth.
> This must seem a pretty speech!—all haste
> And syntaxed with a lover's sighs. Laugh
> If you will—I scarce could answer blame. (52)

After reading *Alfred the Great,* Earle Birney wrote to Gustafson in 1942 (the year of publication of his own first book, *David and Other Poems,* which includes the popular "Anglosaxon Street" and demonstrates Birney's equal fondness for Anglo-Saxon metrical patterns) that "however it would fare dramatically, it fares damned well poetically."[5] As drama the play does have central weaknesses, most noticeably in the pacing, the static characterization of Alfred, and the unevenness of the texture of the verse. Pacing is a problem especially in act 2; the love theme is left in abeyance here, and its omission precludes any relief from the long and rather tedious discussions of the state of the nation. The character of Alfred, dauntless in his endurance of war after weary war fought in the cause of justice, freedom, and fair peace, ultimately lacks dynamism. Alfred's speeches tend to sustain an image rather than forge one. As a stage character, he is curiously passive: his military exploits are reported, not dramatized, and important decisions—such as those concerning exchange and protection of hostages—are taken out of his hands, first by

Elfwyn's unannounced departure for the Danish camp in return for
Ethelred, later by the Saxons' unauthorized murder of Sigurd, who is
not only immensely more vital than the earlier lover Guiscard, but
also a more vividly dramatized character than the play's nominal
hero. While Alfred's "mental majesty" goes undisputed, Sigurd
comes closer to providing the drama's emotional center and to playing the part of its real hero—by his death, almost the role of tragic
hero. The final sweep of the play is not that of tragedy but chronicle,
however.

Gustafson's response to Birney's barbed praise was to assert that he
had not intended *Alfred* as closet drama and that, while the play did
need some tautening, it "should hold up beautifully when spoken."[6]
The careful patterning of sound—one of the major achievements of
Gustafson's mature poetry—emerges first as one of the chief assets of
Alfred the Great. Putting into practice the techniques of Anglo-
Saxon poetry which he had learned during studies at Oxford,
Gustafson creates in this play a strong impression of the stress verse
of the ninth century. This is especially noticeable in the chants of the
old warrior Gar and in the songs of the bard Brand. Gar's opening
speech is impressive in this respect:

>   fierce in fight
> The weary winters, red with war,
> Consume all Wessex, Alfred's might,
> As ashes stifle the flame-log's core.
> Bright was the war-spear, burnished the brand,
> Hard on helm the stark sword rang,
> Grim in grip, hero's hand,
> Keen on corselet steel-shaft sang.
> Many the victories; viking joyed;
> Need then was for the beer-harp's boast,
> Warrior's words, the lithe-tongued song,
> When Ethelred Atheling's might destroyed
> The ocean-goers, Guthrum's host:
> Arrows stung with straight speed strong,
> Vultures vaunted victory-song.
> But now no need for beer-hall boast;
> Barren the land, glutted the coast
> With Dane.... (12–13)

Alfred the Great abounds in alliteration, compounds, and archaisms. Words such as "rood" (Christ's cross), "fytte" (section of a

poem), "skald" (composer and reciter of poems), and "carle" (fellow) recur, their obscurity of denotation more than counterbalanced by the authentic flavor they lend to the dialogue. Proper and place names of the period also contribute to the suitably rugged texture of the poetry. Even the stage directions reveal Gustafson's concern for sound. He indicates where a speaker begins "half-chanting," where "a horn sounds," "the warriors laugh," "there is a roar of laughter," "several spears are clashed on the floor," how people speak "tensely," "quietly," "more quietly," and so on. The reviewer for *Saturday Night* in 1938 hailed *Alfred the Great* as "the first fruits of a new art"—the art of broadcast drama—because "it depends mainly on itself, on its own words and rhythm rather than on its setting."[7]

Gustafson had shown a fondness for consonance and assonance in *The Golden Chalice* which was written, by and large, before he had read Anglo-Saxon literature (or Hopkins); but in the verse drama, the very frequent use of alliteration, coupled with heavy stress and marked caesural pauses, is clearly the result of a conscious effort to recreate the verbal texture of the historical period. Unfortunately, the blank verse line chosen as the standard is not an appropriate vehicle for carrying this independent sound pattern based on stress, pause, and alliteration. Gustafson abandons the iambic line in some speeches, particularly those of Gar and Brand; but repeatedly he finds himself, just for the sake of his pentameter line, relying on poeticisms which bely the earthy tone of the warriors' talk he is attempting to recreate. Expressions such as "acold," "afire," "redoubled back," "aflame," or "'twixt" in the following lines seem to be summoned as a last resort to fit syllabic requirements:

> Swift was the rout,
> The Raven's swoop, as fleet the Viking hate—
> One winter dusk the strength of Wessex! Fled
> Her earls, her people fled. What hope who found
> Them 'twixt the sea and Dane? (59-60)

What is equally strained and awkward about the verse of *Alfred the Great* is the large number of Shakespearean overtones and allusions. Given that the play focusses on a warrior hero, it is not surprising that the chief echoes come from *Macbeth*. Examples are numerous:

> GAR: Would there were no need
> To ask what deeds are done. (14)

ALFRED: The time begs spurs
To prick the stride of its occasion on. (23)

SIGURD: And I'm to cringe remorse
And beg King Alfred's shrift because my maw
Refused to sheathe his henchman's blade? Nor love
Shall wait upon his eminent 'you may.' (78)

INGULF: Look
To the Dane! (103)

ALFRED: Poor need
Of rules to trick our passage from the world,
To quarrel with a candle less or more
To light the dead the way to certain dust. (109)

The lines of poetry are drawn up: Anglo-Saxon against Renaissance, stress verse opposing blank verse. In the last analysis, these two styles have as uneasy a truce as Alfred's Saxons and Guthrum's Danes.

Representing Gustafson's sole venture into the writing of dramatic literature, *Alfred the Great* is an anomaly in his poetic canon in terms of form; yet it marks an important new departure in several ways. First, Gustafson's chronicle play marks a considerable advance in objectivity of treatment, as well as in stylistic competence, over the abstract, ornate, melodramatic poems of *The Golden Chalice*; it is more controlled, varied, and original in terms of imagery and diction, though still derivative and imitative in its unsuitable Shakespearean language. Second, in its alliterative style, Anglo-Saxon diction, and historical setting, the play demonstrates the extent to which Gustafson fell under the influence of Old English literature during that phase of his development covering his residence in Oxford and London in the 1930's. The influence of Anglo-Saxon stress verse on Gustafson, as on Birney, waxes and wanes over the years, but it never entirely disappears from his subsequent writing. Finally, *Alfred the Great* marks a step in Gustafson's gradual shift in thematic orientation away from a Romantic preoccupation with the self towards an involvement with political issues—a movement which culminates in the 1970's in the witness literature of *Theme and Variations for Sounding Brass*—and it holds a significant place in his progress from static early lyrics to the powerfully dramatic style of his later poems.

CHAPTER 3

Poetry of the 1940's: Transition to Modernism

RALPH Gustafson's writing from the mid 1930's to the mid 1940's, culminating in the retrospective collection *Flight into Darkness* (1944), marks a second discrete phase in his poetic development. During these years, he moves philosophically and artistically through a turbulent transitional stage. Losing faith equally in Christian orthodoxy and timeworn literary traditions, he experiences disturbing feelings of fragmentation, disorientation, and apostasy—the state suggested by the title image of this third substantial book. Gustafson's previously unchallenged faith in the goodness of nature, the harmony between human, natural, and divine, and finally the omnipotence and benevolence of the Christian God is eroded piecemeal by his exposure to new beliefs, the depression, war, personal frustration, and loss including the premature death of his mother which terminated a protracted battle with cancer. As he gropes towards a reinterpretation of life involving injustice, suffering, and violence, his poetry expands to encompass themes of disillusionment and existential uncertainty. His style reveals aesthetic ambiguity as well. The poems of this transitional period are characterized by experimentation with new techniques borrowed from the original Modernist writers, and by imperfect amalgamations of older and newer literary ideals.

The first major stimulus to technical change was provided by Geoffrey Grigson, editor of the influential periodical *New Verse* in whose pages other young Canadian poets such as A. J. M. Smith and George Woodcock found publication during the 1930's. Grigson rejected, as static and conventional, work submitted to him by Gustafson in 1932. Gustafson's adult career begins with this rejection for it spurred him to extensive reading of his contemporaries in order

to bring himself stylistically up to date. He had already discovered
Lawrence and Joyce, but now he immersed himself in Eliot, Hopkins,
and the leading poets of the 1930's—Auden, Spender, and MacNeice.
Within a few years, radical new departures in style, diction, imagery,
structure, and theme begin to appear in Gustafson's writing.

The earliest poems to show the effects of his intensive program of
modernization by exhibiting the unmistakable influence of his
contemporaries are "In the Park" and "April Eclogue," dated in their
manuscript forms 8 October and 19 December 1936 respectively.[1]
Even several years later, however—into the 1940's—Gustafson
would on occasion revert to writing conventional sonnets. The beginning of the second phase of Gustafson's poetry overlaps the ending of
the first, and is a transitional period in which earlier Romantic attitudes and traditional forms coexist or alternate with Modernist
themes and techniques. Like the McGill movement poets of the
1920's, Gustafson—a decade later—attempts to modernize his style
by patterning his work on newer but still alien models from
foreign parent traditions; the result is a baroque mixture of voices,
subjects, and techniques. Reeling under references drawn from the
Bible through Louis MacNeice and ranging widely from sonnets to
free verse, *Flight into Darkness* collects new poems and reprints three
slim booklets of the preceding years: *Poems (1940), Epithalamium in
Time of War* (1941), and *Lyrics Unromantic* (1942).

I   Poems (1940)

The eight poems offprinted from the April–June 1940 issue of the
Sewanee Review and bound as *Poems (1940)* deal with war, death,
and love—themes Gustafson had explored earlier but with a different
informing vision of life. In both form and content, these poems reflect
Gustafson's restless, uncertain state of mind as he drifts in a Sargasso
Sea somewhere between affirmative Romantic values and a more
sceptical philosophy.

The most ambitious poem is "April Eclogue." Thematically and
technically it shows the direct influence of Gustafson's self-imposed
program of study of Modernist poets, primarily in this case of
MacNeice and Eliot. It is a modern eclogue dealing with contemporary urban and existential dilemmas which unfolds as a free
verse   dialogue—or   more   accurately   two   counterpointed
monologues—as a poet and another tenement dweller converse at

dusk in the listless London waste land of the 1930's. The man's thoughts turn on pragmatic and routine affairs such as postal delivery, the weather, traffic, and his taking of tea. The poet's thoughts reveal a similar randomness but move to a more philosophical level, touching on death, time, war, love, loneliness, and ephemerality. The musings of both men are sketchy, disjointed, without much logical coherence; this is consistent with the poem's main motifs of purposelessness and dislocation. This portrait of the artist lounging at dusk on tenement steps beside a gutter contrasts strikingly with that given in the prefatory poem of *The Golden Chalice* where the poet posed at dawn on a flaming mountain peak. In every respect "April Eclogue" represents an enormous improvement over the egocentricity, flamboyance, and pomposity of the poetry of *The Golden Chalice.*

The poetry now runs almost to an opposite extreme: portions of the new poem, like the lives of the men it portrays, are pedestrian. The flow of associations is banal; thinking of a traffic jam, for instance, calls to mind jam for tea. In dramatizing the thoughts of *l'homme moyen sensuel,* Gustafson does not find a solution to the perennial problem of how to imitate truly a dull and garrulous discourser without duplicating the actual dullness and garrulity. Then, too, there are contradictions and ambivalences in terms of style. In many ways, the poem is thoroughly modern and imitative of Eliot: its choice of free verse; its experimentation with the technique of free association; its underlying image of the city as a desert land, dusty, barren, and lonely; its incorporation of snatches of jingles, nursery rhymes, and songs, such as "There's no place like home," "Polly put the kettle on," and "Oh to be in England." But archaic terms such as "prisoned" for imprisoned, and precious expressions such as "the swelling volute of the clock" or "the currying fingers/ Of beggars" do not fit with the typically short lines of the free verse paragraphs and their staccato speech rhythm. These faults underscore the tentativeness of this pivotal poem; however, the mood of ennui—even of existential absurdity—and the theme of alienation, which find emphasis in the drift of the monologues and the sterility of the setting, are effectively realized. Ultimately, "April Eclogue" is on a par with early Modernist poems (such as A. M. Klein's "Soirée of Velvel Kleinberger") written by Gustafson's Canadian contemporaries.

The tone of disillusionment and boredom which pervades "April Eclogue" echoes through the remaining seven poems of the 1940 collection. Gradually coming to a sobering realization of the emptiness of contemporary life, particularly in an urban context, and the raw inhumanity of international politics, Gustafson sheds his earlier Romantic optimism. In "Think This No Folly" the persona is stripped of the consolations of the beauty of nature, ruefully acknowledging of the sea and moon:

> Think not these
> A day define,
> Nor that, nor any beauty,
> Anodyne.[2]

Although the suite includes a couple of love poems, fear and uncertainty inspire the more memorable of Gustafson's immediate prewar poems. "Final Spring" begins:

> Of grass, insurgent bud aware,
> We in the loop of sudden spring,
> Trammelled by tangled green and song
> Nostalgic on the ear,
> Thrown by the lariat of sun
> Are branded with initialled fear. (39)

The conceit based on ranching provides an arresting opening for the poem, but it does not match the conventional, sentimental, middle portion of the stanza with its "song/Nostalgic." Like most of Gustafson's poems of this transitional period, "Final Spring" suffers from lack of an integrating force.

The most consistently successful of the eight poems is "Crisis." The tension here between creativity and "the silent/Night"—death—is structural and dynamic; and the solution most characteristic of Ralph Gustafson—love—is proposed. With urgency and solemnity, in nearly biblical rhythms, Gustafson admonishes: "Cherish them now for they shall not be yours" (37). Like "April Eclogue," "Crisis" focusses on the spiritual emptiness of the depression years; its breathless, panicky closing lines acknowledge an irreversible and frighteningly total loss of faith:

> For the word in our time is barren and the deed,
> And the. closing of a gate, we no longer have,
> A friendly door against the silent
> Night and love. (38)

Reviewing *Poems (1940)* and referring specifically to "Crisis," Earle Birney wrote at the time: "Mood and thought are authentic and wedded to our times."[3] This tribute underscores the considerable distance Ralph Gustafson had travelled in the space of a few years.

II   Epithalamium in Time of War

An occasional poem written for the marriage of his elder sister, Pauline Gustafson, to Lieutenant Hector Belton in Newfoundland on 22 March 1941, Gustafson's *Epithalamium in Time of War* is thematically structured along lines drawn by the same dichotomy seen in "Crisis," or earlier still in *Alfred the Great,* between the creative potentials of nature and love on the one hand, and the grim destructiveness of war on the other. The poem is set in England, and through imaginative extension in the betrothed couple's native Quebec, in springtime as the last snow melts and crocuses burst through the earth. The poem hinges on contradictions and para-doxes: the coming of war simultaneously with the arrival of spring; the destructive intellectual power of human beings in contrast to the vitality of nature; the juxtaposition of death and love. An Easter motif unites these antinomies and suggests at least a temporary rekindling of Christian faith that even out of death can come life and, through love, salvation.

While beginning with brief mention of "the warring heart's/Huge anger," the poem presents itself primarily as a celebration of youth, love, vitality, and spring with its bird songs and flowers "And every fraise and freshet torn/With gash and gold that meltings bring" (48). Inclusion of the word "fraise," a term from fortification (meaning palisade), reminds one nonetheless of the war—the backdrop against which the affirmations of the wedding poem stand out. Gustafson notes how nature triumphs despite man's efforts to regulate the universe in accordance with his desires, hatreds, and destructive drives. That the cycles of nature cannot be impeded is not an unequivocal good, however. Man, bent on war, cannot "clap gyves" on June, "manacle morning," or "stop sunward weed"; but equally he cannot prevent his own inevitable decline and death in season. Pharoahs and kings must fall, and even young lovers in the end do die.

War and death feature in this marriage song, but what Gustafson emphasizes is the beauty of union in love. Marriage is presented as the very antithesis of war with its huge hatred, death dealings, and total repudiation of the Christian injunction to love one's neighbor. Underscoring the Easter paradox and relying on specifically Christian imagery ("Sabbath," "boulder," "spike and tree"), the poem ultimately issues in a song of triumph.

> Behold, where drums the day's decline,
> The Sabbath's seven candles lit.
> No cap nor clock nor reckoning,
> No fuse but love shall hallow it,
> No boulder but its Easter bring.
>
> And so to martial hills and holms
> Where Magog holds a town in fee,
> Love's hater, index, darling comes.
> Out of the monster cannon's seed,
> The armoured epoch's gravid wombs
> Make paradox, from spike and tree
> Glad words, read April palindromes! (49)

Despite war and the machinery of war ("drums," "cap," "clock," "fuse," "cannon," "armour"), there is love, happiness, and promise ("seed," "gravid wombs"). The poem ends in ringing affirmation:

> Golden through
> His gates they come! Now belfry, ring!
> Love, them, each living thing, renew!
> To her, to him, His blessings bring! (50)

The style of *Epithalamium in Time of War,* like its theme, is built on oppositions, revealing also Gustafson's shifting allegiances during his period of deliberate self-modernization. The poem is composed of nine, eleven-line stanzas of iambic tetrameter rhyming *a b a c a b a c d c d.* For the sake of his conventional meter and end rhymes, Gustafson is forced into circumlocutions and poeticisms ("watery ways" for oceans), and into inversions of noun and adjective ("crocus green"). Also for the sake of alliteration or rhyme, he dredges up archaisms such as "clavis" (key), "gyves" (fetters), and "holms" (islands). These nouns share space oddly with earthy words such as "sperm" or "guts" and neologisms such as "gale-hardy" or "sky-gallant"—formed presumably by analogy to Hopkins's "dare-gale skylark." In adjacent stanzas, Gustafson speaks in neoShakespearean English of "England's pledge in bosky blow/Where Nightingale her honey puts" and then echoes Hopkins in describing "the plane [which]/Takes drunkenly the field and goes/Gale-hardy, skygallant hanger in blue" (48).

The dominant stylistic influence quite clearly, however, is Hopkins; though archaic at points, the poem is generally elliptical, condensed, and difficult in a Modern if awkward way. Wrenched syntax, ellision of transitional terms, reliance on words which may serve either as nouns or verbs ("manacle," "harvest"), and frequent use of specialized forensic, military, or nautical terms ("writ," "lien," "ravelin," "bollards") combine to create difficulties of interpretation at the level of even literal denotation. The texture of the poetry is overly complicated: sound effects strangle the sense—a fault which recurs in Gustafson's later writing. The effort of comprehension finally is greater than the satisfaction gained from the poetry after the meaning is deduced.

The penultimate stanza of *Epithalamium in Time of War* illustrates this problem. Here Gustafson writes of God's mastery and uses the image of a ship, a combination which recalls Hopkins's *Wreck of the Deutschland.*

> Then take this dear this double love
> Whose loop and lunge on heaven's bollards
> Bind. All love shall Harbour have
> Whose silken nets its fathoms find.
> Nor fear, O let no lover grieve:
> Against the veer and vertical
> Of God the world's vast corners cleave,
> Our pitch and parallel is lined. (50)

Portions of the stanza remain obscure even when the basic imagery is sorted out: love is compared to a rope ("lunge") which keeps one securely hitched to the posts ("bollards") of heaven, like a ship which has found safe harbor. The final lines extend and modify the metaphor: like a ship plunging in a longitudinal direction ("pitch"), Christians have their position marked off with lines on the map of God. The combination "veer and vertical" suggests transcendence, but how do "corners cleave"? Some expressions seem to be determined primarily on the basis of sound, and in general the poetry is too intellectualized. Conrad Aiken summed up his complaints with the poetry by saying that Gustafson had "Hopkins a little too much on his mind, he is determined to make things very hard for himself, and

here we have tortured syntax, tortured order, tortured everything—
anything, almost, if only to avoid the merely straightforward and
formal and simple."[4] But no one else in Canada was writing this
way at the time, and E. K. Brown presented a different estimation
when he judged Gustafson's poem to be "inspired imitation."[5] Even
this more favorable critique, however, admits that the language
is far from original. Gustafson's *Epithalamium in Time of War*
is a work in transition, a personal landmark in formal experimentation, but not ultimately memorable as an independent work
of art.

III   Lyrics Unromantic

Privately printed in New York like *Epithalamium in Time of War,
Lyrics Unromantic* of 1942 is a collection of twelve short love poems
composed in a variety of different forms including free verse. These
new love poems, exhibiting concision and restraint in diction and
imagery, are substantially different from the inflated sonnets on the
same subject published seven years previously in *The Golden Chalice.*
A recurring new theme, in fact, is distrust of words: poems I, III, and
IX are on the topic of the unwordability of love. Gustafson's mastery
of Modernist lyric techniques is revealed in effective short lines,
honed down descriptions, and economy of imagery; indeed John
Sutherland, the controversial and nationalistic editor of *First
Statement,* hailed both Gustafson's *Epithalamium in Time of War*
and *Lyrics Unromantic* as "important contributions to the modern
movement in Canada."[6]

Gradually Gustafson's poetry is becoming more unified, although
the 1942 collection as a whole is still a troublingly inchoate
assemblage of borrowed styles. There are poeticisms—"But we have
made of love/A wondrous use" (65)—and oldfashioned inversions
for the sake of rhyme—"When simple things of loveliness/Inconstant
prove" (56)—alongside surrealistic imagery, syntactical ellipsis, and
condensed parenthetical expressions. Poem VIII, for example, is
heavily influenced by the style and diction of Hopkins's "terrible"
sonnets:

> O love, my love! I, pitched
>   Past durance done,
> How softly do her eyes
>   Hold light, learn. (63)

It should be noted, however, that Gustafson is expressing the agonies and tribulations of secular rather than religious love.

The most accomplished poems are XI and XII, love poems which show clear evidence of greater maturity, both existential and artistic. The long lines of poem XI, "Soon will the lonely petrel," move and hover like the flight of the seabird which is used as a projection of the poet's fear and love, an unusual and haunting combination of emotions. The opening lines are strongly metaphorical as the seabird drifts into the poet's consciousness and becomes one with his innermost feelings or his soul which thereby is stolen away. The flight of the bird parallels the subtle psychological movement towards a realization of love—or is it death? There is also some puzzlement as to how "prophetic/Joy" is to be reconciled with "the midnight's acclamation" and the poet's "fearful thought" (67). Rhythmically, the poem is powerful; yet its full meaning is obscure.

With the partial exception of its middle stanza, poem XII is pellucid and so even more compelling:

> Tenderly, deeply,
> Through the night
> Sleeps my love,
> Violate.

The unexpected realism of the combination "love/Violate" in the opening lines recalls Auden's "Lullaby"; unlike Auden's poem, however, the last stanza does not urge acceptance of human failing:

> Of that we have
> Been certain of,
> Wake innocent,
> My love, my love! (68)

The compassionate understanding of human imperfection, if not its acceptance, and the honest simplicity of diction here are significant new features which prophesy the later strength and originality of Ralph Gustafson as one of Canada's most accomplished and profound love poets.[7]

IV Flight into Darkness

In addition to reprinting the whole of *Poems (1940)*, *Epithalamium in Time of War*, and *Lyrics Unromantic*, Gustafson's *Flight into*

Darkness contains thirty-four previously uncollected poems. Written between 1936 ("In the Park") and 1943 ("Fragmentary"), these poems still are characterized by ambivalence, unevenness, and incongruity in terms of technique and theme. They range in subject matter from conventional landscapes, through current events, to apostatic meditations; in philosophic orientation, from Christian to antiChristian; in structure, from traditional sonnet to experimental forms and free verse. In their totality they demonstrate the aptness of the collection's title, for they succeed in conveying the drift of departure from stability and traditional beliefs on a voyage into a dark night of the soul from which there is no return.

The inability to reconcile the ugliness of contemporary city life with the beauties of nature in large measure accounts for the disputatious quality of the collection and is itself the subject of several representative poems, including the title poem "Flight into Darkness," "Ectomia," and the frequently anthologized, parodic "City Song." The persona of "Flight into Darkness" is clearly citified; he has "turned/Expensive keys against the empty street" and "In evening cities heard the newspaper tossed/Against the door." His own romantic youth, like his culture's, is past. He finds himself "now, regretting June with adult smiles"; but he still rejoices in the "marvels in the township," "that year the tamarack was green," and "The grateful turning-out of lamps at night" (15). Still he can be startled by unexpected glimpses of nature's beauty, so that "coming on sun across/An alien street," he stands surprised:

> As Galileo, before his midnight window,
> Cloak about his shoulders, coldly chose
> A fatal planet—first, listened while
> The solitary wagon passed along the road—
> Then aimed his contradictory lens. (16)

This final image, warmly praised by E. J. Pratt, suggests that the contemporary, urbanized persona who is delighted by simple sunshine is analogous to Galileo whose scientific methods were considered heretical by the church of his day. The new heresy in the depression and war years, Gustafson suggests, is to express abiding faith in the beauty and marvel of the universe.

Tension between nature and machinery structures "Ectomia," too, where again the intensity of Gustafson's images is powerful. The persona laments the removal, excision, ectomia of Romantic vision in our day; "For us no longer is the night/Sharp with the silver grit of stars." Currently the smell of the tamarack is regarded as having "less truth/Than breaks on the bayonet in sun/Word from an automatic mouth." But even through bloodshot, war witnessing eyes one may—by performing a sort of psychosurgery—enjoy "the laughing street/The crunch of stars within the palm/The paunch of sun with mirth grown great" (36). "Ectomia" offers one of the rare happy conclusions in *Flight into Darkness.*

Similarly, conflict between natural beauty and manmade ugliness is implied, though not explicitly stated, in "City Song." Ironically echoing Marlowe's "Passionate Shepherd to His Love," this poem counterpoints the Renaissance pastoral ideal against contemporary urban reality:

> Come, let us take the air
> And stop the bus and pay the fare,
>
> Drink sweetly of the city-streets
> And dream of love on upper seats. (93)

Along with "Psalm 23, Revised Version" (written the following month, in September 1938), "City Song" marks Gustafson's first satiric foray and shows new talents for distancing and objectivity.

As a result of this new objectivity, descriptions of nature in *Flight into Darkness* become less vague than those of earlier collections. A sudden thaw is the subject of one undated nature poem contained in the volume's concluding section subtitled "Of Places and Sarcasm." "Thaw" ends:

> Abrupt, the cables of
>   The landscape lapse,
> The hidden girders of
>   The frost collapse
>
> And like a blast of gold,
>   A clarion,
> A thousand startled waters
>   Take the sun. (74–75)

A still more direct and colloquial attitude characterizes another undated poem "Rebus":

> Daffodils stiff against the amorous wind,
> Fooling the bee with sweet illusion—
> God! how the damp earth smells
> And Marchwind slaps the cheek with cold! (83)

Even in this shorter four-line poem, however, there is a mixing of styles; the dreamy phrases "amorous wind" and "sweet illusion" contrast sharply with the final dynamic metaphor.

Flight into Darkness is marked also by increased social consciousness. One of Gustafson's best known poems of the 1940's is his sonnet "On the Struma Massacre" which commemorates the sinking of the unseaworthy Jewish refugee ship *Struma* in the Black Sea off Istanbul in March of 1942. Fleeing from central Europe, the Jews had managed to reach Palestine; but, because of immigration quotas, British authorities denied their overcrowded and dilapidated ship permission for a landing, with shipwreck and the loss of 769 lives resulting. Though written in traditional sonnet form and expressing Christian faith ("Studied in ignorance, and knowing Thee"), the poem shows the Modernist influence in its frequent sprung rhythm effects. Hopkinsian lines such as "O not those same where, drowned,/Driven by plausible tongues" contrast oddly, of course, with the basic iambic measure and conventional inversions such as "for whom thy Son the tempest bound/And waters walked" (51). But nonetheless, written only a few days after the tragedy occurred, this poem is an important early example of Gustafson's ability to digest political events quickly and to respond with poetry which is topical, a talent hinted at in a veiled way in the political allegory of *Alfred the Great* and brought to perfection by the 1970's, culminating in *Theme and Variations for Sounding Brass.*

Another early example of Gustafson's social commitment and topicality is the more finely wrought and Modernist "Basque Lover" —a poem commemorating an unknown Loyalist soldier killed in the Spanish Civil War. Written in 1937, it is a love poem of a very unusual order: the lover is an eyeless corpse, grotesquely embracing mud and grass. The conflict between Gustafson's Romantic and sceptical attitudes is put at the center of the poem so that his usually uneasy juxtapositions of prosy modern words ("Egregious") with oldfashioned arrangements ("In the mountain-fastness lies . . . /Fatal lover") do not obtrude so disturbingly. "Basque Lover" works on the emotions of the reader by exploiting the hideousness of the cadavre of the Loyalist soldier who, at the same time, is depicted as a young lover. The poem ends hauntingly:

> Beneath the body's lewd embrace
> Twists October's present grass;
> And at the nostrils of the lover,
> Quietly, the wind seeds hover. (35)

The eye-rhyme of the last two lines does not round the thought off smoothly; instead, like the wind-borne seeds, the theme is made to linger and disturb.

Directing his attention to political tragedies produces a fundamental shift in Gustafson's outlook. *Flight into Darkness* for the first time expresses not just bewilderment but also bitterness. Beginning with *Poems (1940)*—for instance in "Crisis"—there are indications of a transition from devout Christian faith to self-doubt and finally disbelief; but in "Ultimatum" (a poem written in November 1938 only two months after "Crisis" although not collected until *Flight into Darkness*), there is a stronger, even despairing, sense of *deus absconditus*. Gustafson's words, like Hopkins's at bleak periods in his religious life, meet a brazen heaven and find no reply. The symbolic blood of Christ thins to common water; on the poet's tongue is not a wafer—pledge of salvation—but dust, death.

> For we are of this time and the body's use
> The workings of the hand are
> Impotent
>
> And on the tongue is dust.
> . . . .
>
> This our need and words
> Sour
> The symbol in our hands water
>
> And there is no reply. (33–34)

Gustafson can no longer believe in an afterlife; the here and now become his sole realities, his absolutes.

> To the sensitive lips the truth
> Within a word between a man and man
> The ploughshare and the earth
> Is ultimatum. (34)

A similar anthropocentric and present-time emphasis is seen in "Excelling the Starry Splendour of This Night," the 1941 poem which opens *Flight into Darkness*. Its implicit antiIdealism is far removed from Gustafson's earlier Christian, Platonic, and Keatsian philosophical outlook. In "Denial," too, the poet is no longer able to rejoice Pippa-fashion that God is in His heaven and that things are as they are. Gustafson's religion, like his style, has been "Pressured in" (23).

Ultimately, however, Gustafson shows no unidirectional growth during this transitional period. His most flamboyant example of Hopkinsian chicanery, "Mythos," a poem anthologized in Eugene Jolas's avant-garde *Vertical,* dates to the same year (1940) as the conventional sonnet "Biography." These two incongruous poems are placed side by side in the untitled opening section of *Flight into Darkness*. The cinematic "Mythos" unwinds in flashes and snatches of color and sound, like a tumultuous dream or impressionistic film. In sprung rhythms and densely alliterated lines, the mythological Icarus is depicted as a man who is

> Staggered, strafed by the sun, dashed
> To glaucous ocean flaming down
>
> Spurt of crimson plunged in foam
> His daring down (Star-dazed dare!
> Hurl then, hurtle the headlong winds
> Nor haggle joy in the gasping lungs,
>
> Moon-managed gallant of gales! Go,
> Greet the giant grapple of sun.) (18)

In point of fact Icarus, son of the mythical Daedalus who built for the Cretan king Minos the infamous labyrinth, is a peripheral figure in the poem. The central character is Theseus, who slew the Minotaur at the heart of the labyrinth with the aid of his lover Ariadne who provided him with a magic ball of thread enabling him to find his way through the maze. Gustafson focusses attention not on Theseus's external victory, but on his inner turmoil (his "mind's snarled labyrinth") as a troubled and uncertain lover. In the legend, of course, Theseus soon deserts Ariadne, who eventually marries Dionysus. After his slaying of the beast, Gustafson's Theseus

> faced
> The giddy exit, frowned. Half-turned
> To her, he heard the distant ocean
>
> Crash its foamy thunder down
> The beach, confused in sun and green
> He thought of marble Athens, mazed.
> Then Ariadne kissed his lips. (19)

Here Gustafson's stylistic mentor—Hopkins—is foreign, and his mythology—Greek—alien; but nevertheless "Mythos" belongs to its time technically and is of interest thematically for its connection to those short stories dating to the same decade which repeatedly depict the turmoil of young men whose love remains unfulfilled.

In startling contrast to "Mythos," the sonnet "Biography" opens with the deliberately archaic line "What time the wily robin tuggeth worm." It then achieves a trimmed, Eliotic poise in groupings such as the phallic euphemism "The cryptic acorn plus the accurate root." Through these stylistic anachronisms, this poem underscores its theme of maturation and affords an interesting double insight into Gustafson's simultaneous sexual and artistic development. Looking back on his youthful Romantic attitude he comments:

> Puberal, still with bended bow did shoot
> Heroic arrows tipped at the fabulous sky,
> Whose silver barbed the snow.

Self-critically, he sums up his adolescent accomplishments. "I, fool, with words of paper, scissors, paste,/ Mailed awkward anagrams to Love and Death" (17). The quality of pastiche is not wholly absent from the poems of his subsequent transitional phase either, of course. But above all "Biography" is memorable—unforgettable—for its explosive final image: "Beneath/ The purchase of my present jaw, I taste/ The apple twixt the tombstones of my teeth" (17). Gustafson's apple, a symbol resonant with connotations of Genesis, innocence, sex, knowledge, sin, and the Fall—in short, the whole of life— wedged between those granite images of inevitable, ubiquitous death, is among the most powerful and thematically central symbols of his entire canon.

Experimenting with a diverse range of sources from the Anglo-Saxons, through Shakespeare and the Romantics, to Modernists such as Hopkins, Eliot, Auden, and MacNeice, Gustafson at times in *Flight into Darkness* reaches the point where his evolving poetic style serves as a more fully adquate and even tentatively original vehicle for conveying the major themes of nature, love, ephemerality, and unjustifiable death. Furthermore these themes, no longer cloaked under conventional Christian pieties, now accurately reflect the temper of their time.

CHAPTER 4

Short Stories: Rites of Passage

THE central themes of Ralph Gustafson's poetry find expression again in his prose fiction. The twin values of "being in love and left free to love"—the words of the central character of one short story entitled "Classical Portrait"[1]—are of supreme importance in both genres. In fact, Gustafson's poems and stories cohere the way musical theme and variations do, together developing an integrated interpretation of experience. The three shared keynotes are creativity, love—whether for the beauties of nature or art, or among man, woman, and child—and strong abhorrence of violence.

Unlike his poems, however, Gustafson's stories generally operate in an indirect manner; they work obliquely towards celebration of a healthy instinct for life and unfettered self-affirmation by probing the distress and human suffering caused by failures of inadequate or blocked passion. In this respect, his short stories are almost mirror images of his poems, their emphases reversed. Contrasts can again be seen on the level of style. Whereas Gustafson's search for an appropriate and authentic poetic style is a slow and laborious process covering several decades, his prose style springs almost full grown from his brow, like Athena out of the head of Zeus. Despite obvious flaws, such as lack of subtlety in conceptualization of plot and character, even Gustafson's first stories—"The Last Experiment of Dr. Brugge," a Poe-like thriller about a mesmerist, and "The Amateur," a biter-bitten tale tracing the crimes of a petty Montreal thief—are compellingly intense.

Dating from the beginning of the 1930's, the period of his arrival in England, is the stylistically sophisticated "Surrey Harvest," of interest for its thinly disguised self-portrait of an expatriate Canadian as well as its rendering of local dialect. The opposition between peacetime farming and warfare, seen also at this time in *Alfred the Great,* is summed up in the modest, but defiant, final line. A Surrey farmer looks up at jets streaking the sky; he spits and says: "Never knewed a

61

piece o' machinery us here now couldn't get the betterin' of."[2] Gustafson's ear for dialect speech patterns and his poet's eye for detail combine to recreate the scene vividly. He depicts the sun with "its gold tangled in the swerve of the hay as it swung on the forks of the men"; the salt as having "escaped through his fingers in a white curve as of snow"; and the clouds as having "thickened near the skyline to a darker colour, opaque with coming rain" (42–43). Details of sight and emotion reinforce each other.

Building from here, Gustafson's prose fiction shows remarkably swift maturation. When he turned to sustained short story writing in the mid 1940's after leaving the British Information Services, Gustafson's work received international attention and acclaim almost immediately: "The Human Fly," published in the prestigious *Atlantic Monthly* in 1947, was then also included in *Best American Short Stories 1948*; "The Thicket" was anthologized in *Cross-Section 1948*, and "Summer Storm" in *Best American Short Stories 1949*; while "The Pigeon" won a short fiction prize from the most important Canadian literary magazine of the decade—*Northern Review*—and was anthologized in Canada, the United States, and Australia. Such critical recognition of Gustafson's prose fiction again is in direct contrast to the essentially tepid reception accorded his poetry until late in his career.

Gustafson has published nineteen short stories; eight of these are collected in *The Brazen Tower* whose publication date of 1974 is misleading: almost all of his prose fiction was written much earlier, during 1946–56 while he was residing in New York City. The familiar lesson that the course of true love never does run smooth was perhaps being painfully demonstrated in Gustafson's personal life in these years; it had already been learned by the ardent young poet-lover of the early sonnets of *The Golden Chalice,* by Guiscard and Ghismond of its title poem, and again by Sigurd and Elfwyn, the tragic young lovers of *Alfred the Great.* The theme is repeated frequently in Gustafson's prose fiction, both in his stories and one unpublished novel, "No Music in the Nightingale," which also dates back to the mid 1950's.

In the early poetry the limiting, negating, disruptive forces which thwart the progress of young love include interpersonal misunderstandings, parental cruelty, possessiveness, and war. Added to these in the short stories—mainly set, like the novel, in the Quebec townships—is the Calvinist-Jansenist legacy of prudery, shame, guilt, and self-hatred leading sometimes even to acts of sadomasochism. These impediments to healthy union between man and woman or parent and child are portrayed with greater complexity and sublety, too, in the prose fiction than in the early poetry since the negating forces now tend to be internalized by the main protagonists.

Characteristically Gustafson's stories, like Joyce Carol Oates's, explore the destructiveness and human suffering which result from people's failure to release themselves to their instinctually positive, creative feelings. The typical Gustafson hero (there are few heroines) remains caged, unfree, and mated with the archetypal Canadian ice woman. His stories document "how one's destiny is the outcome of character," as Jimmy's mother puts it in "The Circus" (53); but beyond this they also reveal how individual character interacts with and is shaped by larger societal influences and pressures. They reflect a postwar consciousness of the human capacity for inflicting pain; they probe the almost subliminal sources of the battle of the sexes; and they also offer very skillful psychological dramatizations of the lingering effects of the puritan ethos on the collective Canadian psyche.

Set in the Eastern Townships, in or near Sherbrooke, even (in "The Pigeon") in the wooden frame house in which Ralph Gustafson grew up or (in "The Vivid Air") on his Uncle John's farm near Waterville, many of Gustafson's stories are thinly fictionalized accounts of his own boyhood. "The Circus," "Snow," and "Summer Storm," for example, are fully autobiographical. Others recount events in the lives of relatives—a nephew's nightmarish experience becomes the girl Deborah's debacle in "The Pigeon," while his own father's approaching death provides the subject matter for "The Tangles of Neaera's Hair." "The Human Fly" depicts an advertising stunt staged by a local Sherbrooke merchant; "In Point of Fact" dramatizes an abortive homosexual pick-up Gustafson witnessed in Venice; it is also tempting in other character studies of men and women failing at love or men feeling emasculated by women, as in "Shower of Gold" or "The Paper-spike," to assume an autobiographical source, whether consciously recognized or not.

The puritanical climate of the townships—indeed of Canada generally as assessed by critics stretching from E. K. Brown in the 1940's to D. G. Jones, Ronald Sutherland, and Margaret Atwood in the 1970's—constrains and compromises virtually all of Gustafson's characters. At best they are shown struggling to loose the stranglehold of the repressive morality which Gustafson himself grew up with and in his adult years tried to escape through self-imposed exile. This morality stresses human insignificance and impotence, equates worldly enjoyment (especially of sex) with sin, and is suspicious and even condemning of spontaneity, emotion, and the arts. In *Survival,* Atwood describes Canadian culture as "the culture of potential denied."[3] In this context, Gustafson's stories paint national as well as regional portraits of human bondage and unfulfillment; thus they contribute to a mainline tradition of Realism in Canadian prose which includes the works of Frederick Philip Grove, Sinclair Ross, Hugh MacLennan, Hugh Garner, Margaret Laurence, and Alice Munro.

In Gustafson's best stories, as in most contemporary fiction, plot and external action tend to be devalued; the main event on which the plot turns may be no more out of the ordinary than a missed appointment ("The Circus"), a casual visit to an art gallery ("Shower of Gold"), or a brief restaurant lunch ("The Paper-spike"). Actions and events tend to be minimal, but the characters' ways of responding endow even minor and everyday occurrences with frightening significance. These are characters who have seismographic sensitivity and heightened emotional and creative capacities: children, artists, and lovers. But typically they are children filled with guilt as they perform the rites of passage into adulthood; artists frustrated by an atmosphere in which aesthetic or sensual pleasure equals sin; and lovers matched with partners who are prudish, vengeful, and even sadistic. The creative person is obstructed in innumerable ways by a society which is fundamentally hostile to his or her self-actualization. The main characters in Gustafson's fiction thus are all victims. A few acknowledge this but refuse to accept the assumption that the role is inevitable, blaming their entrapment on individual repressive sexual partners or specific warped mores. Several of them, however, overwhelmed by a vivid consciousness of the general societal source of their oppression, fail to take any affirmative action—in fact, quite the opposite. There dawns the bitter recognition they are trapped for life by the sterile morality they reject intellectually but cannot shake emotionally, and on account of which they are lashed with guilt.[4]

I   *The Child Protagonist*

In *Second Image,* Ronald Sutherland observes that "whether because of the Calvinist-Jansenist insistence upon original sin or the absence of positive national myths, the typical child in Canadian literature seems· to be born disillusioned. . . . English-language writers are not so obsessed with the tormented child as are their French-language counterparts, but certainly they tend to associate childhood with unhappiness and anxiety."[5] Gustafson's stories about children—all set in Quebec—tend to share the French-Canadian emphasis on psychological torment. The innocence traditionally associated with children is put to rout by an emergent adult consciousness of raw power. His child protagonists in "The Circus," "Summer Storm," and "The Pigeon," for example, all run up against adults who shatter their innate faith in the beauty and goodness of life. What they carry away from these traumatic encounters are lessons in betrayal, cruelty, and violence.

A thinly disguised Ralph Gustafson, the sensitive, stoic, largely misunderstood, and lonely child Jimmy is the focus of narration in two autobiographical stories of childhood—"The Circus" and "Summer Storm," the opening story of *The Brazen Tower*. In both stories, the child's trailing Wordsworthian clouds of glory are severed as blood and violence indelibly etch themselves on his consciousness. "The Circus" describes four year-old Jimmy's sidewalk vigil as he waits for his grandfather—who has forgotten all about him—to take him to the circus. Jimmy's brave patience and silent suffering—his infant obedience to the stiff-upper-lip WASP code of behavior—are rewarded shortly afterwards by the jolted grandfather's establishing a trust fund to provide for Jimmy's education. The sequence of events becomes a treasured family anecdote.

"Summer Storm" is a more penetrating story. Now thirteen, Jimmy is initiated into manhood by performing rites of physical violence which, to his humiliation and chagrin, fill him with irrepressible revulsion and guilt. The story takes place one Sunday out on a lake where Jimmy and his father—whom he idolizes—come regularly to fish, his father finding "more religion sitting in a boat than in the pew of a church" (2). Initially Jimmy admires enormously his father's prowess at the sport and dreams of his own heroic exploits, even at the sacrifice of limbs; but ultimately the story does not celebrate the *machismo* virtues of courage, daring, and defiance of pain. On this particular fishing excursion, Jimmy's mother and sister have intruded on the small Hemingwayesque ritual shared by men and boys, and Jimmy—to his own amazement and shame—finds himself identifying with the perspective of his mother who considers it cruel to allow the caught fish to die slowly in a pail empty of water. When his father vengefully begins breaking the necks of the fish with his hands, Jimmy is disgusted; but his sister's jeers incite him to kill a fish himself in this manner. He struggles desperately so as not to act "scared or sissy" (13); but "an obscure repulsion, familiar, suppressed, slowly emerge[s] into Jimmy's consciousness" (9), and he is overcome with nausea. Parallelling and underscoring Jimmy's turbulence of emotion, a summer storm blows up threatening to capsize the boat. Jimmy finds himself paralyzed and his dreams of heroic action, dashed. The decimation of the fish seems even more horrific and wanton when the bodies have to be thrown overboard so that the pail can be used for bailing. The oars tear his father's hands and become smeared with blood. Jimmy's initiation into manhood has turned into a nightmare of destruction and gore; he struggles unsuccessfully to shut his mind against the full implications of his feelings of revulsion against his father, the broken perch, and the blood.

Written in the immediate postwar period, this grim initiation story with its symbolic depiction of ritualistic violence and senseless killing has a heightened significance. The story resonates with political and also sexual overtones, the fishing rods reserved exclusively for men and boys carrying obvious phallic connotations. That the breaking of the fish can be likened to violent sex is pointed out more explicitly in Gustafson's poem "The Fish," based on the same experience and printed as an epigraph to *The Brazen Tower*. Dating back to 1941, the sonnet precedes the story by several years and affords a different perspective on the event. The poem sardonically records the boy's resolve to kill the fish rather than leave it to die slowly; the speaking voice notes ironically that the boy looks away as he commits the atrocity. The tone of the poem establishes that the event is being described by an adult accustomed to destruction. The story, however, is given greater psychological impact by being presented from the point of view of the sensitive pubescent boy who is just coming to a consciousness of the violence of the adult world. The boy's sensations provide a more compassionate moral barometer than adult logic, so that the differences between the story and poem underscore an important contrast in child and adult outlooks on life.

This contrast is reiterated in a very different context in the recollection of an idyllic northern childhood "Snow," a quietly moving story narrated by a man who obviously regrets having left behind him both his boyhood and the Canadian countryside. He longingly remembers the blue snow of winter, his enchanted snow-house, and sugaring-off. The opening of the story is virtually a prose-poem, combining realism and poetic description:

. . . all through the hours the white flakes would come down, small and hard and delicate, making a sifting sound in the air and a brushing on the sides of bankings and trees and bushes and sills. Stopping in the night on the sidewalk, you heard the flakes fall, touching the earth with a whiteness and the edges and wires and footprints of the area around you with a deepening and a susurration; and high in the night, above the reflection of the lamp, filling the air with a falling without beginning, peaceful and unhastening so that you were held, for the minutes you were lost from your purpose and heard nothing but the storm, between a feeling of wonder and far regret and of death and a love that was missed and could be, the flakes came, tangled in your sight and falling on the world and the folds of your scarf and on your eyelashes so that in wonder you put out your sleeve and looked down before the crystal on it could vanish: a symmetry and star beyond all use and science and retrieving. You were caught between time—and unable to endure, remembered your purpose and adulthood and losses and moved on, thinking of the roads tomorrow, and practical things to be done and picking your way uncertain of the sidewalk beneath the fall of snow.[6]

Impossibly perfect snowflakes which fall, break, and vanish symbolize the path of human destiny (as again in two later poems, "And in That Winter Night" and "The Overwhelming Green"). The story goes on to tell how the young boy curses his mother and falls from pristine innocence, sullied by guilt.

"The Pigeon"—one of Gustafson's best stories and certainly his most successful—again is concerned with rites of passage. As in "Summer Storm," the killing of a living thing, a portion of nature, is presented as the necessary act of initiation into maturity. In this case, the ten year-old child Deborah runs up against her callous father who embodies the worst aspects of North American manhood. He inflicts his *macho* values on Deborah to a point where she feels incompetent and inadequate simply because she is a girl; she grows apologetic for not being the desired son who would share his father's ruthless outlook on life and enjoy virile pursuits such as hunting.

Left alone one night, Deborah befriends a pigeon who has strayed into the attic of her house. She offers it milk and crusts of bread, crooning over it and telling the bird "I love you!" (79). These gestures bespeak both her loneliness and her loving, gentle nature, while the poetic language in which Gustafson records her musings further suggests her sensitivity. "Perhaps it was thirsty and was drinking the velvet white milk that made no sound with its silvery bill and the rainbow around its throat" (80). But Deborah knows it is wrong for her to be up in the forbidden attic in the first place; and her uneasy,

guilt fired dreams push her into the rash decision to set the bird free
that night before her aggressive father finds and shoots it. In her
attempt to liberate the bird, however, Deborah inadvertently causes
its death amidst crashing photographic plates: the bird is impaled on
broken glass. Later when Deborah sees her father with the bleeding
bird in his hands, hatred for him sears her innards even though she
outwardly surrenders hysterically to his image of her as nerveless
and incompetent. Again the spilling of blood carries connotations of
both war and sex, symbolizing the child's dual awakening into a
consciousness of power and violence as well as sexual identity. Guilt
floods over her as she comes to a horrified realization, finally, of "the
wrong things that were not her fault that they happened" (84). Thus a
conviction of sin becomes real for Deborah, as for the child of
"Snow" and for Jimmy of "Summer Storm." Even while it is clear
that these children will never concur with adult insensitivity, they are
forced to cross irreversibly out of the realm of childhood innocence
and naivety.

II   *The Artist Protagonist*

The frustrated artist, as well as the guiltridden child, is an
archetypal victim in Canadian and other literature. In Gustafson's
writing, the experiences of the sensitive and imaginative child grappling with family politics too callous for her or him to cope with
successfully seem in fact to form a paradigm for the frustrations of the
artist who confronts an equally stunting, much larger social group.
The effects of a puritanical, socio-religious hostility towards the artist
are studied in several of his stories, including "The Thicket" and "The
Vivid Air," as well as in his novel "No Music in the Nightingale."

The plight of the artist in the townships—which form a microcosm
of Canadian society—is broached first in "The Thicket" through
Gustafson's portrayal of the painter Richard, brother of the central
character Maria. Richard resembles Philip Bentley, the failed artist
of Sinclair Ross's 1941 novel *As For Me and My House*, although
Maria for her part struggles wildly to reject the role of martyr which
Ross's Mrs. Bentley wears like a badge. Richard is inhibited from
asking a girl whom he has admired in the market stall next to his
father's if she will model (presumably nude) for him. Describing the
girl in the market, Richard reflects crudely: "Enough flesh—yet bony
enough. Do you think she'd model? Enough sex in it to make me draw
with guts. Solid."[7] Maria refuses his request to intercede with the girl,

partly because she is jealous of the attraction this woman holds for her brother, and partly perhaps because she intuitively rejects the demeaning stereotype of woman-as-object. Richard is angry with Maria for her refusal to cooperate and lashes out, shouting "how the hell can you expect to do anything in this place" (50)—a rhetorical question resonant with echoes and implications throughout the history of Canadian literature.

Maria's own predicament is still more complex, and on her characterization hinges the value of the story. Unfortunately Gustafson's depiction of his prime character is mired in chauvinistic stereotyping of the "castrating bitch" whose real villainy is her refusal to submit to exploitative, male sexual demands. But although flawed and therefore not selected for inclusion in *The Brazen Tower,* this story holds considerable interest. In its sexual symbolism, its insistence on the primacy of the libidinal drive, and its depiction of the possessive and sexually inhibited woman whose life will be radiantly transformed if she is rescued by a man, "The Thicket" shows D. H. Lawrence's strong influence on Gustafson. Maria is kin both of Miriam Leavers and Mabel Pervin.

Maria rejects explicitly the example of female bondage afforded by her neighbor, Mrs. Simpson—"scorning the stupid secret in Mrs. Simpson's flesh that bound her to Mr. Simpson" (49)—and implicitly, the example of feminine submission of her dead mother. Yet, enmeshed in a society which offers her no viable alternatives, Maria seems doomed to relive her mother's life; in order to please her widowed father and her brother she now keeps the family home precisely as her mother had arranged it, "dishes, food on the same shelves, used at the same times. Her father was made happy" (49). Still, Maria is a passionate woman with an artist's eye for sensuous details, such as "the cache of captured sun—where the path turned farther from the road, where she sat inviolate, fiercely alone—the ferns, sensual and exquisite under her fingers; the coarse bark against her flesh; the smudge of tiger-lily pollen on her palm" (49). Indeed, it is insinuated that she retreats to the thicket not only to read—which she does ravenously—but also to masturbate. Gustafson's conclusion, which presents Maria as longing to be raped and forced into submission by a man, therefore is false to her passionate if compromised spirit of independence.

Ultimately Maria is far more disastrously a victim of shackling societal pressures and restrictions than Richard, although Gustafson does not attempt to engage sympathy for the woman's plight.

Whereas Richard feels thwarted as an artist by the puritanism of the region which reduces his effectiveness in painting human anatomy, Maria is prevented from aspiring towards any career outside her own home by constraints that limit her possibilities to the traditional female roles of dutiful daughter, domestic drudge, or surrendering mistress and wife. Richard's repeated complaint that "this is a hell of a place anyway. If you want to do anything" (51) seems petulant and whining next to the unvoiced frustrations of the woman who has no creative outlet at all for "the power that was hers—a waiting power" (51) and who consequently steers her life on a self-destructive course.

The life negating ethos of the townships is explored again in Gustafson's gripping, psychological study "The Vivid Air." Like his poem "All That Is in the World," the story launches a virulent attack on Christian attitudes. Its central character is the artistic Abel Fast, an adolescent who has been brought up to believe that kissing, poetry, music, and drink are all sinful. As he comes to manhood, he attempts to rebel against this puritan legacy; but his efforts are doomed to failure. While Abel's father and stepmother are away at the Synod in Quebec City, Abel goes to the Chautauqua, a travelling entertainment from the United States which includes performances of the balcony scene from *Romeo and Juliet* and "The Overture to William Tell" with "The Storm" by Rossini. Giving himself over to the sensations of the orchestral sounds filling the Chautauqua tent, Abel comes to the conviction that beauty and sensuousness are not sinful but sacred. "He knew once and for all that sensuousness was not sinful, that to hold richness sacred within him was right."[8] The music of "The Storm" leads up to a literal thunder and lightning storm in the same way that the stage representation of love urges Abel to end his virginity by consummating his sexual desires with Elly, the hired girl back home. He realizes "Elly was what the music was about; not Elly, he did not mean, but the living-out of life, of the possession of the music and the notes that were set down, the glory and the use" (14–15).

At home Abel's passionate resolve wanes; but he chastises himself for cowardice until, reaching the point of entering Elly's bedroom, he discovers that another man—Dread Nordstrom—is already with her. Out of a combination of anger, humiliation, and guilt, Abel masochistically jams himself in the wood-cording saw in the barn, vowing to cut off one hand in expiation for his lust. Elly and Dread stop him just in time; but then in a frenzy of sadistic anger and guilt, Elly, picking up a halter, begins to whip Abel—catching his thighs and making his hands bleed—while she screams out rhythmically "Damned Jesus! Damned Jesus!" (19). Distortion of life because of repression of sexuality thus is graphically sketched against a background of natural beauty uncontaminated by human intellect as dawn breaks. The story joins the poem from *Rivers among Rocks* in "damning those who roar/Delight and sin, equation" (poem 7).

Abel's inability to release his passion satisfactorily—an inability stemming partially from his unshakable though unconscious conviction about original sin, which then grows into a crippling sense of guilt—typifies a main concern of Canadian writers. In Ralph Gustafson's writing the church as a force opposing the pleasures of the senses and the encouragement of the arts is repeatedly attacked—in the humorous story "Heaven Help Us," in his novel, and in poems such as "On the Top of Milan Cathedral," "Churchyard near Treuchtlingen," "The Great Day," "My Love Eats an Apple," and "At the Pinakothek Ruins: Munich." Ultimately for Gustafson, expressing love through art and sex is one indissociable creative act.

The links between love and art are underscored by the very title of his unpublished novel, "No Music in the Nightingale: An Ironic Comedy," which is borrowed from Shakespeare's *Two Gentlemen of Verona*; "Except I be by Silvia in the night/There is no music in the nightingale" (III, i, 178–79). This theme is exemplified in the life of the poetic young lover Brand Dorset, the novel's main figure. He is the last descendent of the family who founded Lime Rock (the fictionalized Lime Ridge, Quebec) at the time of the migrations of the United Empire Loyalists following the American War of Independence. As a young man, he gives up his study of law in Montreal to reestablish himself on the last remaining piece of the family property, beside Mirror Lake. He has discovered that the city is "ugly and inquisitive and successful" and that "most of the law was illegal and that what living was for was music."[9] In returning to the township valley of the St. Francis and abandoning his career in the city, Brand manifests again "the crazy poetry of the Dorset blood" (6) which has already lost most of the Dorset lands to the calculating Bradshaws.

Brand is neither liked nor accepted by the people of Lime Rock. They remember how his widowed mother, the beautiful Melissa Dorset, nonplussed by their opprobrium, had brought the boy up in a hotel after her husband's suicide; they seem intent on personally visiting the social sins of the parents upon the son and so are scandalized when Brand falls in love with Ann Bradshaw, the daughter of his own father's hated enemy. (In fact, Henry Bradshaw soon undertakes to drive Brand off the last of the Dorset properties in order to exploit their sulphur resources.) But in essence it is Brand's—the Dorsets'—sensuous and independent character which really has antagonized the narrowminded and puritanical townspeople.

Any Anglican of the Parish might have known—except that it was beyond the powers of any Christian imagining—what would come of his carryings-on at the church social with Henry Bradshaw's daughter under Henry Bradshaw's own nose until Henry paraded out. They had spent at the least twenty minutes in the carriage-shed before returning to waltz publicly. . . .

His behaviour was a reminder of the composition of Dorset blood to the whole county. What they couldn't understand . . . was Ann Bradshaw's astounding conduct in accepting to waltz with him in the first place—though it was known to Goodness that she had hung around with a pit-worker all evening and was now the owner of an automobile. The ultimate foundation of it all was the completely radical upbringing of Ann in the United States of America by Marion Broughton since the death of poor Alice Bradshaw. Beyond that, it was, of course, the fact which no one till her dying day would get over, of Melissa Dorset living over a saloon for ten years when she could have had the charity of any one of them. If the outcome had not been what the whole of Lime Rock could have predicted, one would have seen the hand of God in the scandal. (131–32)

This self-righteous smugness frustrates Brand's simple desire to return to the land he cherishes and court the woman he loves. Although his character is neither drawn in fine detail (is he after all a poet or a musician? what is his fate in the end?) nor well counter-pointed against his friend and rival for Ann's love, Johnny Gulbranson—a pit-worker who aspires to be a photographer and who accidentally blows himself up in an attempt to save Brand's lands—the novel does succeed in developing a brooding, claustrophobic atmosphere of scandal, shame, guilt, and hostility to ecstatic self-affirmation whether through love or the arts.

III   *The Lover Protagonist*

Some of Gustafson's most interesting character studies involve what appears, on the surface at least, to be a conflict between repressed, puritanical woman and instinctive, creative man. Gustafson's male characters for the most part are creators: poets, painters, artists, architects; but the typical Gustafson woman has neither productive professional career nor fulfillment through children. The love of which these women are capable characteristically is depicted in negative terms—inability to abandon themselves without shame or guilt to sexual passion, undemonstrativeness, lack of emotion and sexual feelings. These negatives, perversely, are esteemed as feminine social graces. In short, the typical Gustafson woman is an ice goddess who epitomizes "stunted or doomed fertility, the identity of birth and death."[10]

Barbara in "Shower of Gold" seems as cold as Arctic ice to the young architect Chris who is obsessed with the desire to marry and impregnate her. "He pushed the breath in his nostrils out. Imagining her being aware of him was equivalent to the South Pole discovering Amundsen. Or was it the North Pole Amundsen got to? Anyway, ice" (112). As she makes her self-absorbed way through the Metropolitan Art Gallery in New York, Barbara's slim, suited figure contrasts unfavorably with the voluptuous, yielding women of Titian and Georgione. She seems to find her counterpart, however, in Tintoretto's painting of Suzanna, the apocryphal figure who resists adulterous advances of lascivious elders. While the biblical story holds Suzanna up as a shining example of marital fidelity, Gustafson's Chris reinterprets "Suzanna the paragon, whose virtue if laid bare was lack of emotion. . . . Or was he thinking of Barbara?" (113). Chris has been rejected and demeaned in several ways: Barbara has turned down his proposal of marriage; she takes him for granted; she has humiliated him sexually. He prefers to see the roles of the sexes in Miltonic terms, quoting to himself the lines: "For contemplation hee and valour form'd;/ For softness shee and sweet attractive grace" (113). Chris angrily remembers how "he had gone to her apartment, once, at her asking. To make love to her at her asking. He found her sitting, her knees clasped shielding her, the sun of the bedroom window across her. He asked her if she was sure she wanted him. She did and he had stripped and she had compared him to her Great Dane, Loki. He had lost his readiness. Bungled. The need of her had begun" (119). His love, then, and overwhelming "need to impregnate her" (111) amount to little more than an obsession to prove his sexual potency. Repressed anger boils under the lid of his WASP politeness; "the compulsion knotted in him—to strike her, the flat of the palm of his hand across her cheek striking her" (115).

Chris is almost predictably enthusiastic about Titian's painting of *Danaë*. Exuberantly he tells Barbara the legend of how the seven-times married and much philandering Zeus impregnated Danaë in a shower of gold semen to produce Perseus; at this time Danaë was locked in a brazen tower by her father because of the prediction that his own grandson would kill him: "He told her of Danaë locked in the impregnable tower, and Zeus, descended in a shower of gold . . . the legend of heaven and earth, and of both whose moment was reality and whose passion was fixed in the dust and the gods and determined. She listened, the opulence of the passion of the Titian encompassing her: Danaë nude and manifest, her hand halted from shielding her from Godhood earthbound and inexpiable and made manifest in the shower of gold—as he would pour into her the seed of him" (118–19).

The Brazen Tower takes its title from this legend whose central image is emphasized by the illustration accompanying "Shower of Gold": a stylized depiction of the sun (traditionally associated with the male deity Apollo) pouring down and entering a moon shape (the female Diana) trapped between phallic protrusions, the symbolic tower which is Danaë's—woman's—prison. Gustafson's sympathies in "Shower of Gold," as in "The Thicket," do not lie with the penned and ravished woman, however; Barbara is indicted as an unresponsive and castrating bitch.

"The Paper-spike" is thematically similar to "Shower of Gold." Set in a quick-lunch restaurant at noon, it studies the relationship of a reserved businessman John and his bashful, submissive wife Judith. The conjugal life of John and Judith is unfulfilled in passion despite the legal sanction on the act of sex between them. John resents his wife's passivity. "Even the beginning—wasn't it?—had been the same. Tender, submissive, his own passion sensuously blind to the fact that never once had Judith sought what she accepted. Nor since. All of it had been something to be got through—gently, with love for him— but got through" (89). In elliptical, coiling lines of thought (which present some of the same grammatical complexities as his poetry of the same period, although to a lesser extent), Gustafson's protagonist lays most of the blame for their failed relationship on his wife's asexual nature. But her evasiveness and reticence have a socio-religious basis, as John realizes: "the tolerance—the avoidances— what was the whole of it but Judith innocent? himself innocent? victims of a leftover, halfbaked puritan brew of Pleasure Is Sin whose two thousand years left Genesis the Devil's; *Creator castratus.* He'd take the poet: *All absolute sensation is religious*" (90).

Gustafson's John is citing his namesake John Keats as another stick with which to beat down his wife's moral barricades; yet John's emotionally constipated nature makes him, in his own way, reticent and undemonstrative. For example, John responds to his wife's gift of suede gloves with no more than a mumbled platitude, and similarly buries his feelings about his morning's business success. When John asks him eagerly about the renewal of an important contract, John bottles up his elation and describes his morning in one word: "Usual" (93).

Judith shows signs of severe repression and inhibition; after ten years of marriage, she is still embarrassed to receive a kiss from her husband in a public place. But John's demands for affection from his wife are excessive. As he sits waiting for her arrival in the restaurant, he is in a state "imperial with what he knew would happen. Her eyes turned—discovered him—trumpets tilted, as though spring had driven up through the snow outside" (92). The phallic connotation of the last image underscores the male chauvinism of a character who subconsciously sees his relation to his wife as analogous to that of imperial power to adoring, submissive subject in need of his protection. John's bullying attitude to women in general is shown further in his cynical speculation on how the cashier must act in bed and again as he snaps his fingers for the waitress, gives her his order, and thinks that "the girl . . . was grubby, and what was worst, courageous" (93).

John's manhood, like Chris's, is somehow threatened by women. He seems hedged in by his judgmental wife opposite him; the indifferent, rabbitlike woman devouring lettuce on his right side; and the saucy cashier with the rubber bosoms on his left. His repressed desires filter into his consciousness but are never articulated, and he imagines a parodic crucifixion in which he demonstrates through self-sacrifice and blood his passion which has had no release in marriage.

He opened his eyes. The paper-spike stood, cold, pointed, on the edge of the cashier's booth, behind the low glass partition. He moved in his imagination, as if he had; reached over to its passion. He placed it in front of Judith in the centre of their table—the paper-spike that was failure and meaning; to her, of no hurt. He opened his palm rigid above the spike—then struck down.

The spike pierced, came through the back of the hand. The blood clung smoothly the oval base to the quickening pool.

His hand impaled, he told her quietly, "Don't you see, Judith? I loved you, I loved you?" (94–95)

But in the end, like Chris, John keeps his polite facade in place. He leaves the restaurant with his wife without giving his feelings away.

Nicholas of "The Human Fly" is the one Gustafson protagonist capable of breaking the spell held over him by a sadistic ice woman and of expressing his deep emotions by gesture, if not words. Nicholas has become engaged to Louise after coming home from the war, invalided. But despite his association with war, Nicholas is a sensitive and gentle person whose fiancée puzzles him. "As he now stood protecting and holding Louise he again found himself questioning her. He sensed that she was unaware of him, that she was not sharing his feeling that the crowd, the whole morning had taken meaning when he put his arms around her" (30). But Nicholas, having more insight than either Chris or John, realizes that "perhaps his need for expressed affection, his unsureness of himself, made him too demanding" (30).

Louise, for her part, resembles Barbara and Judith in some ways— she hates crowds and dislikes to be touched, even by Nicholas. "Submission to her own elaborate terms was the almost impossible fee" (26). This particular morning, however, Louise has insisted that they join the crowd watching an acrobatic feat—a cheap advertising stunt in Nicholas's view—on the storefront of Boulanger's Hardware. Louise's absorption in the stunt annoys Nicholas, just as Barbara's absorption in the paintings annoys Chris. Nicholas believes that the acrobat, the Human Fly, with the lettering on his back stating BOULANGER'S BUYS ARE BEST, must be capable of better things than this sensation mongering. As Nicholas watches the Fly and his gaudy, indifferent wife, the thought strikes him that this man is foolishly and hopelessly entangled in an unworthy love. That the situation between stuntman and wife parallels that between himself and Louise, Nicholas at first denies; but in the end his intuition is confirmed. As the Fly is poised in a handstand on a rocking chair on the rooftop, his wife—for no apparent reason—grabs at the table which holds the chair, and her husband arcs over the edge of the building. "He fell with ridiculous ease. A small apostrophe in slow-motion, upright, in control, that enlarged into the hurtling twisting figure of the Human Fly. The sound of the impact filled Nicholas' belly with nausea. He had heard such a cry as the Fly's before—under barrage" (36–37).

Nicholas attempts to protect and shelter Louise from the gruesome sight; but sadistically attracted to the bloody scene, she shoves him away from her. His love, already strained, suddenly snaps. "Turning against the surge of people, he viciously fought a path away from her" (37). This story, like the others, searches through the psychological detritus of the battle of the sexes to present a drama of human need and its unfulfillment; but unlike the others, "The Human Fly" reaches a decisive resolution when the angry and disappointed man drops his chivalric mask and acts in accordance with his instinctive feelings. The outcome is a tortured and final split.

IV   In Coitu Inluminatio

The short story which concludes *The Brazen Tower*, "The Tangles of Neaera's Hair," comes extremely close to the thematic heart of Gustafson's poetry, not obliquely but directly. This one story alone speaks of love and fulfillment between man and woman, though its structure provides an ironic double hook: the loving protagonist is an old man, a widower who hobbles about his hospital room with a silver pin in his broken hip, knowing that the hour of his death is not far off.

"The Tangles of Neaera's Hair," Gustafson's most mature and sensitive story, moves with grace and dignity in and out of the old man's mind, articulating his values and his fundamental beliefs about life and death. The narrative is studded with symbols, such as birds, flowers, and sundial—objects which the old man sees outside his window. The brilliantly colored yellow warbler, other birds in the garden, and water in the bird bath are embodiments of the life force. "The birds came and disported themselves in the bath on its cement pedestal; preening and ducking, showing off the glints of colour caught by the water and the sun; leaving in a sudden instinctive acceptance of danger, and returning to the rim, cautious then forgetting, flinging the waterdrops from the surface under their wings" (126). Juxtaposed with these images of life is a *momento mori,* a sundial. "Beyond them, apart from the foliage, stood the square sundial stuck with its acute-angle iron stylus. Around the metal was written the motto, *I alone am constant*" (126).

The old man does not fool himself that love and beauty last forever or even that these experiences are wholly free from failure and pain; but, like Thornton Wilder in *The Bridge of San Luis Rey,* Gustafson indicates that the love will have been sufficient in its way. So although the old man is losing his hold on life (walking to the washroom, for example, is now a major accomplishment), he rejoices in the peonies and lilacs outside his window and recalls beautiful moments shared with his wife, who had died slowly in continuous pain years before. Inevitably he has to accept the reality that "all things at generation moved toward death" (127). He admits that "his dying would pull deep out of life. He was still profoundly alive enough crazily to hate death" (131). But he is not bitter; rather he celebrates passionately the ephemeral sensuous universe for as long as his strength lasts. The theme of "The Tangles of Neaera's Hair" can be summed up in a phrase of Johnny Gulbranson's from "No Music in the Nightingale": "he understood the irony: the ordinance to praise and the death required" (80). In the story, though the old man is dying, "he rejoice[s] at the hedge of April lilac. And the scent of the peonies at the sill. For all his elegies, man answered the flash of the wing" (128). This is the central theme of Gustafson's mature poetry, too, most particularly of *Fire on Stone* and *Corners in the Glass*.

The symbol of the flash of the wing yokes together two antagonistic realities: transience (symbolized by the brief instant, a "flash") and beauty (the "wing" which recalls the vividly colored birds at their bath in the garden). The old man provides a gloss when he muses that the flash of a wing was the sign that Neaera, one of the many women in Greek mythology loved and impregnated by Zeus, could be "brought to bed" (127). Neaera appears again in Milton's "Lycidas" where she is associated, like Amaryllis, with eroticism. "Were it not better done as others use,/To sport with Amaryllis in the shade,/Or with the tangles of Neaera's hair?" (11. 67–69). The flash of the wing and Neaera's tangled hair are richly resonant symbols. Together they represent the complex intermingling of love, beauty, fertility, nature, and art.

This story, written within a few years of Gustafson's marriage, belongs to the period of many of his finest love poems. It offers a paean to life, natural beauty, and above all woman, as lover, wife, and muse. Neaera's tangled hair calls to mind specifically the image of the old man's beloved wife who had danced with an upside down mop long years ago as if she were a reincarnation of the siren who "comes from the blue water to fill the silence and the loneliness of the world with song" (132), and who later near death had lain with "her hair . . . spread on the pillow" (131). This sequence underscores the Janus-headed reality the old man embraces: love and death.

Exploring psychological and physical violence, sexual frustrations, guilt, and failed human relationships, Gustafson's mid career prose fiction expands the range of his work. But although his stories characteristically work in an indirect manner—as exposés of puritanical hostility towards physical manifestations of love through both sex and art—the ultimate conclusion of his prose fiction, like that of his poetry, is an affirmation of the greatness of spontaneous and free expressions of love in this sensuous, sublunary universe. The stories depict a series of frustrated lovers and trammelled creators. But always implicitly, and in "The Tangles of Neaera's Hair" most emphatically, that which is underscored as being of the highest value is love. *In coitu inluminatio,* a phrase from Pound's "Canto 74" which crops up in Gustafson's poetry at this same period, is the solution to the complex of *creator castratus* which his fiction presents.

CHAPTER 5

Poetry of the 1960's: Heir of Centuries in a Country without Myths

THE third and most interesting phase of Ralph Gustafson's career as a poet effectively begins in 1960 with the publication of *Rivers among Rocks*, and it includes the seven books which in increasingly rapid succession have followed: *Rocky Mountain Poems, Sift in an Hourglass,* and *Ixion's Wheel* in the 1960's; *Selected Poems, Theme and Variations for Sounding Brass, Fire on Stone,* and *Corners in the Glass* in the 1970's.[1] Gustafson's third substantial book of poems, *Rivers among Rocks* collects his work for the sixteen-year period 1944–59, the time when most of his prose fiction was also written. As has been outlined in Chapter 4, in his poems and stories the major emphases tend to be exactly reversed; whereas the fiction typically dramatizes human unfulfillment and inhibited creativity or sexuality, the poems are a more direct and affirmative presentation of the joys of beauty and mutual love.

Gustafson's development as a poet from the 1920's to the 1960's provides a miniature history of Canadian literature, moving from outdated imitation of Romantic/Victorian nature poets, through a transitional phase of similar dependency on the early Modernists. Now, free from the exaggerated Keatsian decoration of *The Golden Chalice* and those awkward verbal assimilations and amalgamations of poets from Hopkins to MacNeice which characterize *Flight into Darkness,* the poems of *Rivers among Rocks* experiment with a more authentic and independent style. (Significantly, this is the first of Gustafson's books to be published not by a foreign publisher, but by McClelland and Stewart in Toronto.) Unlike his abstract earlier work, Gustafson's mature poetry depicts sensuous life in vivid, vital detail. He manages to present "the testimony of the actual"[2] in a way which renders lived experience both concrete and also symbolic, so that his style tends to illustrate—by embodying it—one of the major

80

themes common to both his poetry and prose fiction: that the transcendent, the highest meaning of life, is to be attained not by denial, but rather by affirmation, of temporal realities.

I   Rivers among Rocks

Rivers among Rocks (1960) takes its title from the Book of Job: "He cutteth out rivers among the rocks; and his eye seeth every precious thing" (28:10). Confrontation with the godhead in order to reach an understanding of the place of the human individual in the universal scheme of things provides the point of departure for these poems which are arranged in three discrete sections, each given its own epigraph and illustrated with powerful graphics by Canadian designer Frank Newfeld. The first section collects the most densely metaphysical poems; in philosophical and religious language they present an essentially intellectual response to the same recognition of mutability which had struck Gustafson before, though less forcibly, in *Flight into Darkness*. The second section groups poems which give his emotional response as lover to transience—a response which includes anger, defiance, and protest, as well as love and joy taken in the world of the senses. The concluding section gives his aesthetic response as poet; this response centers on celebration of the beauties of the Quebec landscape and classical works of art which attempt— like poetry—to translate the impermanent beauty of the natural world into more enduring form.

That the first section of the book is highly speculative is suggested by the very titles of some of the fifteen introductory poems—turgid and legalistic titles such as "Prolegomenon at Midnight" or "The Disquisition." Gustafson, like Job, is searching for truth; unlike Job, however, he will not rest content with the consolation that true understanding can never be found in the land of the living and that the highest wisdom, therefore, is fear of the Lord. His attitude to life has swung radically away from Christian faith and Romantic optimism; this is reflected in his poetry which is now disputatious, antiKeatsian ("Unheard music is not sweeter"[3]), and even antiChristian.

"All That Is in the World" (poem 7) is one of the more accessible of the difficult introductory poems. Angry, bitter, and anticlerical, this poem takes its title from I John 2: 15–16: "Love not the world, neither the things that are in the world. . . . For all that is in the world, the lust of the flesh, and the lust of the eyes, and the pride of life, is not of the

Father, but is of the world." As is demonstrated also in the short stories of this same period (most notably in "The Vivid Air"), renunciation of the sensuous aspects of life is perceived by Gustafson as an intolerable negation. This poem lashes out vehemently at the exhortations to abstinence issued by John, Paul, and other saints or churchmen who "given flesh, ungraced it" by preaching sin, martyrdom, and rejection of the sensuous world (who, figuratively, "The tangible rose/Oppose"). According to Gustafson, their outlook is crippling, unhealthy; he is "Sick, sick with it!" For him: "Than Zion is,/This autumn's more persuasion,/This maple, more."

By orthodox Christian standards, Gustafson's beliefs verge on the profane; but he systematically rejects the traditional icon of the cross, symbol of suffering and sacrifice. He creates a personal, secularized religion instead, celebrating natural beauty—here the maple tree and its perishable leaf whose vivid autumn coloration provides him with intimations of the eternal. "Such present praise and glory/Throughly thrust/This dust." The highest human achievement, then, is not the faith in the Lord that the Book of Job stresses; rather it is a passionate commitment to sensuous beauty in all its temporal manifestations. Illumination of the meaning of life comes to Gustafson through loving and enjoying—not renouncing—the things that are in the world. Repeating Pound, Gustafson sums up his quasipantheistic position with the words "*in coitu inluminatio*"—through physical love, through coition, comes enlightenment. In "All That Is in the World," as in the short story "The Tangles of Neaera's Hair," and throughout his later poetry, Gustafson worships the here and now. It should be noted, however, that, although some of his poems (particularly those of *Flight into Darkness*) exude the despondency of one who believes the godhead hidden, Gustafson is no atheist and never denies the existence of a deity.

In a seminal 1961 review article assessing *Rivers among Rocks*, Louis Dudek suggests that Gustafson's literary father—not just in terms of style, but also in terms of theme—is Hopkins. But whereas Hopkins's primary devotion is to spiritual reality, though sensuous delights constantly tempt him, Gustafson's principal dedication is to the world of the senses, though the spiritual dimension of life is not ignored. Dudek observes that for Gustafson the absolute "manifests itself only in the actual, the real, the world of the senses; and this provides the central theme of the book *Rivers among Rocks*."[4] Gustafson's religion is a secularized one celebrating the glory of things of time; ultimately his mature poetry, like W. H. Auden's or

Wallace Stevens's as well, is offered as a sacrament of praise for all that lives in the world.

This conclusion is reinforced by other speculative poems of the opening section of the 1960 collection: the preliminary discourse of "Prolegomenon at Midnight," the more elaborate investigation of "The Disquisition," the meditative poems "At the Ocean's Verge" and "Legend," and the tripartite "Triptych for an Ancient Altar" which closes section one. In "Prolegomenon at Midnight" (poem 2), Gustafson suggests that love and poetry are the only appropriate responses to ephemerality. Knowledge of limits should make us ardently embrace the beautiful and lovely objects of this changing world. The only solution ("solver") of the human predicament is love ("that daredown doter"); keeping our sights on this target is our one hope for hitting upon the meaning of life: "What only solver but that daredown doter/Launched like a lackluck whose heroics, none/Of our laurel, target love?"

The less Hopkinsian language of "The Disquisition" (poem 6) is easier to comprehend. In this poem, Gustafson attempts not merely to present but to embody his philosophy; words for him, as for Heidegger, have become the unique dwelling place of being. He writes that "Nothing is that is/Not stated"—highlighting that language is one with sensuous experience—and later that "Reality is the expression of it" (poem 29). Joy in this sensuous universe leads him not to praise the Creator, as it did previously in "Magnificat" of *The Golden Chalice*; it moves him to celebrate the concrete objects of the sublunary world. These tangible, visible realities are the primary manifestations of God, and those who suppress or deny the evidence of the senses—intellectual eggheads, sexless ciphers, and morbid ("hipped") churchgoers—are soundly reprimanded. "The Disquisition" rejects Idealism—refuses, in fact, to consider the idea as at all separable from its physical expression:

> all
> 's a rhetoric in the mind
> Until ice burn the wind,
> Until love is in bed,
> Breath out of head,
> Until stone crush worm,
> Until John Plowman is warm.

The one Christian saint for whom Gustafson maintains respect is Francis of Assisi who, loving the physical creation ("A robin and an

ass") shunned "austerity/In a cave." Piety and abstinence are
presented as false guides to salvation and immortality. Puritanical,
WASP Sarah Maudes lie under gravestones as inescapably as the
Helens; but a Helen—a person whose beauty and love become
legendary—more nearly achieves immortality since her passionate
story lives on in art, myth, and history. Reflecting on human history
and confronting the problem of mortality, Gustafson comes in the
final lines of "The Disquisition" to a recognition of the supreme value
of human love, the love of man and woman in its urgent, physical
sense: "History wakes in him only/The need to hold Helen." As he is
to do with increasing regularity in later volumes (especially in *Sift in
an Hourglass*), the Gustafson persona—a very thinly masked figure—
presents himself as a gravedigger who "Digs in tomb to accost/
Cleopatra's dust." Yet an awareness of the brevity of life rouses him
not to lament the incontrovertible fact of death, but to celebrate
beauty and love—the fullness of transience—in this sensuous,
mutable world.

In his mature poetry, then, Gustafson has a double vision, a
simultaneous realization of the beauty and the brevity of life. "A love
of life and the brevity of it," he notes. "Put the two together and
you've got pain with no end. Yearning."[5] But Gustafson's mature
poetry is neither self-indulgent nor self-pitying. His secularized
religion is affirmative and outward looking, his philosophy more
than a hedonistic *carpe diem*; he is neither reckless of consequences
nor forgetful of death.

One of Gustafson's favorite images for depicting the conflict
between time and eternity or transience and permanence is the
shoreline. The place where sea meets sand reminds him equally of
birth, generation (water), and death, erosion (sand). While walking
along the shore, the persona of "At the Ocean's Verge" (poem 4)
becomes intensely aware of fecund, various life:

> fig-trees,
> Snow, macacos, ocean's hurl
> And surf and surge, on applebough
> As crag whose cave holds kraken or
> With comb of coral mermaid cuddles.
> All's mad majesty and squander.

He is also reminded of impermanence by the lonely, level sands—
minute fragments of eroded rock: "The sand is miles and packt/And

moonlights wash the gnawings of/A million years." The ocean's verge is a suitably ambiguous image for rendering intelligible in poetic terms Gustafson's paradoxical, secularized religion; in many of the same nouns, adjectives, and verbs as in this poem, it had already been conjured up in the earlier "Mythos" of *Flight into Darkness*. "Mythos" concludes as Theseus turns from the Cretan labyrinth to face

> the distant *ocean*
>
> *Crash* its *foamy thunder* down
> The beach, confused in sun and green
> He thought of *marble Athens,* mazed.
> Then Ariadne kissed his lips. (19)

"At the Ocean's Verge" picks up these key words, concluding: "Hear how this *ocean* thurls and *thunders!*/*Crashing foams* and ravels once/Was muted *marble Athens* owned." This poem does not end, like the earlier one, with a lover's kiss; but the movement from renunciation of the world to a passionate embrace of it is underscored by a comparison of its opening sentence, "I should pray but my soul is stopt," with the sensuous richness of the language and imagery of these lush concluding lines.

Again in "Legend" (poem 1) which opens *Rivers among Rocks,* the persona at the sea's side feels the silken sand underfoot, imagining "what's left/Of Helen naked drag between his toes." Though "doomed" himself and recalling that "Ilium toppled"—knowing, in other words, that all human achievement is unstable and in a state of flux—the persona still centers his thoughts on symbols of dangerous beauty and love: Aphrodite ("shell and seafoam" recall Botticelli's famous painting of Venus's birth), Circe ("her of Aeaea"), and Helen. "Legend" thus repeats the movement from recognition of mutability to passionate celebration of passing beauty and love which is characteristic of Gustafson.

His philosophy is clarified by the three poems of "Triptych for an Ancient Altar" (poem 15) which concludes section one. These three sonnets, composed during 1944–45, in fact are the earliest poems in *Rivers among Rocks* (barring the revised "Prelude I" which had appeared in *Flight into Darkness*). In the first poem, "Parable," Gustafson's persona confesses his agnosticism by describing himself as one who "has not Daniel's charming prayer"—that is, who lacks that unshakable faith in God which saved the biblical Daniel from death in the lions' den. The persona thus does not expect to be saved from "relentless" death; he instead "Must end up meat within a winding gut." But as a poet he has words which, through a process far from logical ("What damnable logic is upon me proved?"), form neither a prayer nor a curse before the recognition of imminent death; they shape instead a passionate celebration ("That meets this lethal beauty with furious praise"). The boulder is shoved against the exit, and no Easter miracle is anticipated; still, despite his doom, the persona celebrates the beauty of this dangerous, death-bound world.

"Fable," the second sonnet, rejects the idea of bargaining for immortality like Joshua did who stopped the sun and moon in the valley of Ajalon; "Apologue," the third sonnet, explores transience, alluding to Jonah who, after coming out of the whale's belly, was given a gourd for overnight shelter. The gourd was destroyed next morning by a worm. Something that so quickly perishes is a natural symbol of transience. The persona concludes then that "taken joy is all"—the same conclusion reached by the old man at his life's end in the story "The Tangles of Neaera's Hair." He acknowledges the brevity of human life but also its paradoxical greatness, for it is man who names God as master: "I would be mortal, elected darkness, starred,/That I as necessary, make you, Lord." These strikingly anthropocentric lines from "Apologue," which recall Gustafson's earlier poem "Excelling the Starry Splendour," conclude section one.

Section two begins with "The Meaning" (poem 16). The first word of this poem is "so," suggesting that a conclusion has been reached which allows the poet to move beyond the probings and questionings of the highly disputatious opening poems. He is now fully committed to embrace like a lover the impermanent world of the five senses:

> So I, who love, with all this outward
> Now have done, upon each sense
> Has purpose inned, the five are sermoned,
> Meaning is a prevalence.

Although he endorses the life of sensations, Gustafson is no longer Keatsian; nor is he an orthodox Christian. In the second section of this volume, he is still searching for his proper place in the universal scheme; but the quest for meaning is conducted now (without apology or explanation) neither in the terminology of rational discourse, nor Romantic philosophy, nor Christian dogma, but rather through love—of woman and natural beauty. *Rivers among Rocks* in fact contains some of the finest of Gustafson's love poems, composed during the late 1950's at the time of his falling in love with Elisabeth (Betty) Renninger, whom he married in 1958.

The title of one of these love poems, "The Election" (poem 17), carries theological overtones referring to the choice or preference for predestined salvation of certain people over others. For Ralph Gustafson, prefiguring Leonard Cohen, lovers are the only immortals, but even their transcendence lasts only for Browningesque infinite moments. The persona in this poem sifts through the wreckage of history—Carthage, Rome, Athens, Nineveh (whose king Sardanapalus mentioned in the penultimate line was notorious for decadence and luxury)—and finds in the feats of civilization no greater permanence than he finds in the blue of a robin's egg or the perfection of a lover, nude. In a contemporary review, Ian Sowton singled out for special praise this love poem, which "superbly transmutes the dusty multitudinous history of humanity into the moment of private sensuality."[6] "The Election" celebrates the heightened, ecstatic moment of eroticism and love which is thereby rescued from what Gustafson in a much later poem calls the "total/Damned mathematics"[7] of each mortal's numbered days.

That Gustafson's ultimate religion is a religion of love is demonstrated even more clearly in another very fine love poem, "Beach with White Cloud" (poem 19). The conviction that the transcendent is attainable only through the sensuous explains the use of religious imagery in this and several other of his love poems. Accumulating simple suggestive details like an Impressionist painter, stroke by stroke, Gustafson in "Beach with White Cloud" uses the traditional Christian symbols of blood and bread in an unorthodox way:

> The rage touched
> Your knees, thighs.
> Blood broke, bread,
> Stone, skies.

The Christian symbols celebrate a sensual communion and become sacraments in a profane religion which praises the carnal objects in this world, the corruptible body of love, flesh and dust.

Because Gustafson's double vision hooks both the beauty of this world and its brevity, even his love poems frequently are either elegiac or defiant in tone. Gustafson's persona in "Armorial" (poem 3) ponders what images might compose his heraldic arms. His colors would be red ("gules," "bloodred") and gold. He and his lover might be represented by stained red "leopards/Passant on bars of gold." These contrasting colors, like the two discrete strands of imagery with which the tapestry of the poem is woven—one based on English history and the other on geography—underscore Gustafson's doubleness of vision: this poem, like the earlier wartime wedding song *Epithalamium in Time of War,* yokes together love and death. The imagery includes flowers ("roses," "lilies," "rod and bloodred weed and rush"), and other living, moving creatures ("leopards," "larks," "porcupine") and embodiments of the life force ("water," "field"). But still the persona is stalked by death. Roses remind him of the Wars of the Roses in fifteenth-century England; the porcupine strikes an image of the arrow-riddled Richard III who was killed by the Earl of Richmond (later Henry VII) in the 1485 battle which ended the Wars of the Roses at Bosworth Field; the lily is also ambiguous, having Lawrencean overtones of sexuality ("She lay down with love and my hand/Was gold with dust of lily") and equally of death—Richard falls twisted in a ditch "His hand wristdeep in lily." But it is not only love and death that are counterpointed; Europe, with its historical pageantry and famous buildings is subtly contrasted with Canada, a country "Far from kingdoms, which regal grew," "A field without myth or rhetoric." Gustafson's heraldic coat-of-arms, like his vision of life, combines several fundamental contraries; and "Armorial," an elegiac love poem, concludes with the poignant line "My love wept."

The epigraph for the middle section of *Rivers among Rocks* is again from Job: "Canst thou draw out leviathan with an hook?" (41:1). At this stage, Job has become thoroughly convinced of the ignorance and helplessness of man vis a vis the monster of chaos, the godhead, and the universe at large. But unlike Job who grows despondent, Gustafson protests against accident and death. Another love poem is entitled "Monstrance, in the Face of Malign Accident" (poem 23). In manuscript it begins, "Betty, let's love;/In defiance of it."[8] The final version is more abstract, removing the personal element and the conversational tone of the draft; but clearly still the solutions to the human predicament, to the fact of mortality, are love and rage—a Dylan Thomas-like refusal to go gentle into that good night or a Yeatsian clapping of the hands for every tatter in the mortal dress. Gustafson concludes that "This deathwatch/Asks an anger."

Although death and disease may be real, so too are the wine-red clouds of sunset and the snowy throats of women. "This Love is Not a

Praise" (poem 24), which immediately follows, reaches an affirmation despite the horrors of cancer and radical surgery. "Your eyes/ Are mine. I note/ They are not out." What gives the individual significance and meaning in life, what establishes importance in human history, what alone allows one to defy mutability, is love, even if blended both with sadness and anger. Section three has for its epigraph the line from *Romeo and Juliet*: "O flesh, flesh, how art thou fishified" (II, iv, 38) where Mercutio playfully mocks Romeo's changed condition as a lover. That love is the right response to the human dilemma is stressed again in the poems of this concluding section—not just love of one person for another, but also love of nature and art.

Gustafson's persistent engagement with the realities of Canadian rural life and wilderness begins memorably with the poems of place collected mainly in the third section of *Rivers among Rocks*. He celebrates the "local heart" (poem 32) in poems such as "Quebec Night," "The Blizzard," "Quebec, Late Autumn," and "The Blue Lake"—poems which in simultaneously concrete and symbolic ways explore the geography of his native land. Depicting the Canadian landscape, Gustafson now notes with authenticity the sharp, irrefutable details of the northern land under the impact of swiftly changing seasons. In "Quebec, Late Autumn" (poem 43) he speaks of how

> Suddenly now the ragged oak
> And maple overnight are fire,
> The green sluice falters in the elm,
> The ribs and roots of storage fail.

And he notices that

> Now in the barnyard steams the mound
> Of straw searched shiveringly by hen,
> The zinc pail holds a hoop of ice
> Standing in the milking stall.

A relentless, harsh, cold land is portrayed in a curt, economical style. Gustafson's language is direct, simple, solid, "Like fieldrock brown/ Against the turning blade" (poem 20). In 1957, writing his introduction for the *Penguin Book of Canadian Verse,* Gustafson had noted a different intimacy with nature in comparing English or American poets with Canadians such as Pratt, Smith, or Birney, for in Canada "there are no places for yearlong thought in green shade. . . . We are hitched to the seasons—four sharp ones with no south to melt into. After ice-lockings, we dive into spring. Conditions are good for spare lyricism, metaphysical wit" (30–31). The cool, spare terms of poems such as "Quebec, Late Autumn" illustrate this stringency in Gustafson's own writing.

Beauty, peaceful if stark, is depicted in many of his nature poems. An ominous power, however, lurks just beneath the surface in some of them, even those set in a more auspicious season than autumn or winter. In "The Blue Lake" (poem 41), for example, the central image of a black pike which hangs in shadow just under the surface of the water is a symbol of death inextricably twined into the life process. This summer poem elicits, if not terror, at least mute recognition of human powerlessness against the forces of nature and death, for the black pike lurking in shadow is not greeted, as are Daniel's lions in "Parable," with "furious praise." Although the pike, like the biblical lions, is easily understood as a symbol of death, it is not similarly part of a spiritual tradition in which man through God prevails. Forming part of the physically powerful and ultimately indifferent terrain of Canada, the pike has no figurative connotations or historical associations of transcendence. The poem forms a single sentence beginning "I see." The adjectives are stark: "white," "blue," "clear," "black." In keeping with the theme and the mood of the landscape, the style too is bare, reduced, and exposed.

The last section of *Rivers among Rocks* includes poems not only about Canadian rural life but also about art—the writing of Vaughan, the sculpture of Epstein, the music of Debussy, Ravel, and so on. Like the eighteenth-century Viennese composer Christoph Willibald Gluck, who actually moved his clavichord outdoors to compose in the fields (poem 40), Gustafson moves farther and farther away from "heavenly fields" in an effort to make his art more responsive to his immediate environment; but again like Gluck, he by no means abandons tradition—literature, art, history, mythology—while taking up his position "under the sun." The dichotomy between what Eli Mandel has termed "an almost primitive feeling for place" and a "cultivated literary awareness"[9]—a dichotomy Mandel finds in several contemporary Canadian poets—is one of the chief characteristics of Ralph Gustafson's mature poetry. Gustafson is alternately a new Canadian Adam taking his green inventory and a hoary traditionalist—in Michael Hornyansky's words, "the heir of civilized centuries," living in what Gustafson refers to as "a country without myths."[10]

In using the sensuous to reach the transcendent, Gustafson's contact with physical reality sometimes is made directly with things in nature; at other times, indirectly with their representations in works of art—poems, paintings, tapestry, music, sculpture, or other artifacts. It is interesting to note, furthermore, that when Gustafson depicts the natural world, he writes almost exclusively about Canada; but when he describes the world of art, he writes almost always out of a European cultural context. He has two very different sources of imagery in his nature and art poems, then, and with them develops two distinct poetic styles. In the sense in which Northrop Frye used these terms in his famous "terror" review, Gustafson's poetry may be either "aboriginal"—drawing its inspiration from the land—or else "original"—returning to cultural origins through study and imitation of poets and other artists of the past.[11]

Examples of Gustafson's "original" writing can be found in "Four Songs for Antiquated Music" and "Six Preludes." The first of these four songs (poem 40) is subtitled "Lament for the Romantics." In it Gustafson mourns the passing of famous lovers—Romeo, young Werther, Troilus, Cresseid. The poem is antiKeatsian, its last stanza stating unequivocally "Truth and Beauty die." But, sharing the wisdom of Robert Frost that earth nonetheless is the right place for love, Gustafson continues:

> Truth and Beauty die.
> In the ilex grove
> Helen is
> For having love.

"Six Preludes," influenced by music and perhaps also by Eliot's *Quartets,* unite not only literary tradition and classical mythology but also sculpture ("Prelude I" was originally dedicated to Sally Ryan), art (a Picasso lithograph inspires "Prelude II"), and even tapestry ("Prelude III" responds to the fifteenth-century French tapestry "The Hunt of the Unicorn"). In the latter, in order to recreate authentically the activity and the garb of chivalric huntsmen whose custom it was to use ground-up unicorn horn as an aphrodisiac, Gustafson chooses suitably medieval language: "In chamlyt slashed and gardid ciclatoun/ For very courtesy yclad." In the poem, as in the Tournai tapestry which is its source, the fleeting world of nature and human passion presumably has been transmuted by artistic alchemy into more permanent form; but art and language themselves, as Gustafson's quaint style subtly underscores, are still subject to considerable deterioration or change in time.

Gustafson's preludes are very polished linguistically and structurally; yet there is a certain precious, enclosed quality about them for they are reflections of reflections. Gustafson's own rewordings, too, draw off energy and color. "Prelude I," published first in *Contemporary Verse* in 1941, revised for *Flight into Darkness* then for the *Fiddlehead* in 1954, and revised again for *Rivers among Rocks* in 1960, initially presented a clear image:

> What are you about,
> White faun, finger
> Up, phallos
> Nestled in thighs'
> Black curls?
>
> Hoy! Bronzed boy slanting sun—
> Leap!
>   Split blue![12]

In the poem's early reworking, the graphic adjectives "white" and "black" are replaced with the vaguer terms "false" and "caprid." Two other revisions, however, are improvements: the static verb "nestled" becomes "slant" and "slanting" is correspondingly changed to the more engaging and dynamic "tilting." The new version runs:

> What are you about,
> False faun puzzled
> There, phallus
> Slant in the
> Caprid curls?
>
> Hoy! bronzed boy tilting sun—
> Leap!
>   Split blue![13]

Further revisions modify "false" to "dud," "phallus" to "stiffener," "slant" to "lax" and, worst of all, the vivid "bronzed boy tilting sun" to the flat "wrong reckoner." The sum total of these progressive revisions is to rob the poem of dynamism and clarity. In *Rivers among Rocks* (poem 39) it reads:

What are you about,
Dun faun puzzled
There, stiffener
Lax in the
Caprid curls?

Hoy! wrong reckoner—
Leap!
Split blue!

As Fred Cogswell pointed out at the time, Gustafson's style is confined here "within the very real limitations of *preciosité* and imagism."[14]

In its entirety, then, *Rivers among Rocks* ranges from the intellectually astringent, through the passionate, to the aesthetically refined and rarefied. Some of the poems are unsuccessful, derivative, confusingly elliptical; but the majority are subtle, resonant, and technically accomplished. One contemporary reviewer summed up that "at times he strains for a spareness of expression and an involved structure which can almost dehumanize his thought. But basically he is a very human writer."[15] This apparent contradiction points to a very real dichotomy in Gustafson's writing; still, this collection—the first of his final phase—holds a distinguished place in the Gustafson canon.

II   Rocky Mountain Poems

The craftsmanship of the art poems of *Rivers among Rocks,* fusing to some extent already with the simplicity of the nature poems, shapes the style of *Rocky Mountain Poems.* This collection of descriptive and speculative nature poems, published by Klanak Press in Vancouver in 1960, tests the implications for the writer of living in Canada, "a country without myths," a place without a long history of achievement where "all is a beginning," a land without artifice, pageantry, and historic national symbols, "Without tapestry and coronations, kings crowned / With weights of gold."[16] These eighteen poems (selected from a manuscript sheaf of thirty written between 3 August and 10 November 1959 on location primarily in the spectacular Alberta and British Columbia mountains between Jasper and Revelstoke[17]) depict the harsh, massive, overpowering terrain of the Canadian Rockies and Gustafson's responses which include awe, humility, self-directed comedy, and reverential love. They form a series of impressionistic monologues in which the poet-narrator articulates his vision of nature's magnificence and strength, his understanding of the relation of human life to this unchartable Canadian wilderness, and his sense of inadequacy for recreating in words such ineffable, nonhuman beauty.

Awed by the immensity and power of the Rockies, Gustafson initially tries to capture the magnificence of the setting in its total otherness by relying on general, abstract terms. The result is an earnest but vague descriptive passage such as this from "Into the Tonquin Valley":

> The Ramparts, the greatness cragged
> And broken, lying on the mind
> Until the mind gave in,
> Creation only itself,
> Vast, tumultuous. (11)

Part way through the first poem, he reasserts the man centered conviction expressed earlier in poems such as "The Disquisition" and "Dr. Johnson Kicks Hocking's Shin"; nature is said to be the product of an active mind—a fundamentally Romantic notion. Gustafson refers to "the magnificence/That was there, that did not exist/Until we beheld it" (11). The poem goes on to trace how the emotions of the perceiver change, cancel, and create either magnificence or terror as he moves first in a spirit of confidence and adventure, later a state of panic and physical discomfort, along mountain paths or through a trailless maze of mosquito-breeding muskeg, brush, and bog. The poet-narrator concludes: "There is no unconferred/Majesty in peaks" (14). Like Pratt in *The Titanic* or Birney in "David," Gustafson searches out man's place in the universal scheme, attempting to comprehend his relation to nature which seems, despite his metaphysical efforts to yoke it to human consciousness, vast, primal, and unconquerable. The poem ends without reference to human life: "Stone last in the sun,/Scrawled by life of the sea."[18]

While the forces of nature are immensely potent and indifferent if not designedly destructive, the forces of human imagination, will, and devotion are equally significant in Gustafson's view. But his typically anthropocentric emphasis at times now seems inappropriate, laughable. In "Contrary to the Grandeur of God," Gustafson deflates through wry humor the pretentiousness of thrasonical man challenging God and nature. Quickly humbled by the mammoth landscape, the poet-persona recognizes that the Rockies are "immeasurables" (24) and that "On mountains/One does not try out metaphors" (13); therefore he turns his attention to smaller, more manageable portions of landscape—"treetrunks/Trimmed the sun to dazzle, we tripped/On ragged dapple" (24). "The Walk in Yoho Valley," in which these lines appear, provides a harlequin contrast to "Into the Tonquin Valley." In other poems as well, Gustafson describes the magnificence of the mountainscapes obliquely rather than directly, with comedy and humility, as he closely observes small details: a hummingbird in "In the Valley of Wenkchemna," a flower in "The Single Delight," strawberries in "The Trail Under Mount Michael," and pine needles in "Over Toward Mystery Lake."

But this alien terrain will not mirror his reflection. Margaret Atwood's Susanna Moodie suffers a similarly devastating experience in the untamed Ontario wilderness of the nineteenth century. In this respect, Gustafson's *Rocky Mountain Poems* can be compared usefully with the *Journals of Susanna Moodie* or with Wallace Stevens's "The Poem That Took the Place of a Mountain." Stevens describes the process by which the poet attempts to recover a sense of personal or national identity by finding his roots in the natural environment, discovering "Where he could lie and, gazing down at the sea,/Recognize his unique and solitary home."[19] The behemoth of the Rockies stubbornly refuses to yield up to Gustafson his desired human reflection or any clues about his identity, however. The brute beauty of Takkakaw Falls (which also inspires one of Earle Birney's poems) baffles the persona; contemplating the cannonading water—a traditional symbol of life—he is led relentlessly to thoughts of death. A series of "it should" clauses indicates his inability to reconcile himself to the rugged, indifferent power of the Canadian wilds: the falls "should have slope/to the sea"; "it should have grace/till it slips there"; "it should have canyon"; and "it should slope/like river" (22–23). But this terrain obdurately offers sheer cliff, not gentle slope. English Lake District poetic conventions do not apply; only those of Anglo-Saxon stress verse or of Hopkins's rugged sprung rhythm seem to provide a model for grasping and recreating this jagged, uncivilized beauty. Just as the Canadian Group of Seven artists had to abandon European conventions and techniques to portray adequately and authentically the vibrant, bold colors and lines of the northland, the McGill movement poets and here Ralph Gustafson develop a honed down style to fit what A. J. M. Smith in his famous poem "The Lonely Land" terms "the beauty/of strength/broken by strength/and still strong."[20] The experience of a decade or more of prose writing, the experiments in the simple, spare poems of place in *Rivers among Rocks,* and the dictates of this immense, alien geography of rock and ice combine to produce a terse, chiselled, elemental style.

Gustafson devises neologisms to capture the unique qualities of the untamed land. Compounds such as "snowpeaks" and "rocktons" suggest solidity and strength; they remotely resemble Anglo-Saxon kennings, words formed when the English language, like the Rocky Mountain chain, was in a primitive condition. Though unusual, the experimental language is not obscure for the most part and the disjointed syntax creates an effective verbal repetition of the jagged, assymmetrical beauty of the land. But occasionally Gustafson's subject fits awkwardly into an Old English pattern. The snow tractor in "On the Columbia Icefield" and the airplane in "On the Yukon Run," for example, belong too obviously to the era of modern technology to be contained, except ironically, by archaic forms. Although one or two poems read like low pitched travel diary entries ("On the Flanks of Carnarvon," "Over Toward Mystery Lake"), Gustafson's attempt here to create a solid, granitelike linguistic structure stripped bare of verbal ornamentation—similes, extended metaphors, even accumulations of adjectives—is highly successful. In fact, *Rocky Mountain Poems* was distinguished with a Borestone Mountain Poetry Award in 1961. In "The Walk in Yoho Valley," Gustafson makes a remark which can be applied to the style of the finest poems in this collection: "Trail-marks were good,/This being complex country" (25).

Two of the most satisfying poems, "At Moraine Lake" and "In the Yukon," express the contest between geography and history which is a recurrent and central motif in Gustafson's mature poetry. That the nonindigenous Canadian poet must locate symbols in the land rather than human history is underscored either explicitly or by implication in these two poems which move from recreation of a personal experience in the massive landscape to metaphysical speculation. "At Moraine Lake" begins simply enough with the poet-narrator reflecting on his experience of climbing Mounts Hybla, Babel, and Quadra, and of hiking near Consolation and Moraine Lakes (all in the region of the celebrated Lake Louise). But his mind moves beyond the immediate environment when flowers in his cabin summon up thoughts of Circe, and boots set out to dry suggest to his imagination the wanderer Odysseus. The incongruity of the two chains of associations strikes him: one is based on Canadian nature, the other borrowed from Greek mythology. Yoking together the two storehouses of images produces the absurd juxtaposition "Philomela/Snowbound."[21] In fact, the inappropriateness of legendary Mediterranean figures in the context of Canada illustrates the point Gustafson had made earlier in the introduction to the *Penguin Book of Canadian Verse* where he noted that "there are no Aphrodites in Canadian poetry—the seafoam is too cold. The Furies have to be imported. The Laurentian Shield is the intruder" (30). So, alluding to Aphrodite, he writes in the conclusion of this poem: "Take her of the foam somewhere where/It's warmer." With an important pun on the key word "lie," he dismisses imported myths that "Lie about us in our infancy," directing attention instead to something alive and tied to the earth—the ants. The poem ends: "Look, I am occupied with/The irrevocable decisions of the ants" (19). The distortion which occurs when a foreign culture is transposed from a mother country to a new land—the typical colonial dilemma—thus is confronted. "At Moraine Lake" deposes European traditions and replaces them with a more authentic spirit of place, what Gustafson in another poem calls "an elsewhere/Crazy, nearer look."[22] This emphasis on place links Ralph Gustafson, at least in his "aboriginal" poems, with other contemporary postcolonial writers such as Derek Walcott, Wilson Harris, and Patrick White; and it suggests his animadversion to his myth making Canadian colleagues associated with *Alphabet* in the 1960's. In a recent letter, Gustafson wrote: "I suppose we belong as much as anybody to Jung's horde of stored-up universal myth. . . . But all that has been better done elsewhere. One gets fed up with Reaney and Co.'s 'Alphabet.' Instead of playing with coloured blocks on the floor, Canadians are much better occupied with observing what the ants are doing."[23] Critical studies of Canadian literary tradition in the 1970's—*Butterfly on Rock, The Bush Garden, Survival*—stress the supreme importance of the myth of the land itself; and throughout *Rocky Mountain Poems* Gustafson's writing shows the extent to which he confronts the realities of place. Figuratively he has

> pitched
> gloves off, touched
> cleanly
> the green ice
> the green fire.[24]

"In the Yukon," the final poem of the Rocky Mountain collection, is a less overt argument about Canadian identity and
relation to the land than "At Moraine Lake." It is structured
on the polarity between civilization (Europe) and wilderness (Canada). The poem begins with a statement of contrast between
Europe's time honored traditions and the lack of this historical
perspective in Canada. "In Europe, you can't move without go-
ing down into history./Here, all is a beginning" (36). Instead
of historical engulfment, what Canadians have is geography, nature.
The grandeur of this country, Gustafson suggests, lies in its natural pageantry of flora and fauna, not in the realm of human
struggle and achievement. Canada is a green world, not the or-
namental gilded one of European ceremony and artifice. The
poem records the cycles of birth and death of the Pacific salmon,
the passage of the seasons from summer to fall, the movement
from day to night—all natural phenomena. It ends with an awe-
some depiction of the north with its ineluctable, alien, lonely
beauty, and ultimately that gravity of death: "the north/Going
to what no man can hold hard in mind,/The dredge of that gravity, being without experience" (36). "Mind"—knowledge, logic,
reason—is not the faculty to uncover the final truth of nature.
Intellect is insufficient; spiritual or sensuous experience is necessary. One must embrace the mystery, the power, and the physical
realities of place.

Gustafson's personal and national quest for identity, for a right
relation to the land, for what Stevens calls "the outlook that
would be right/Where he would be complete in an unexplained
completion,"[25] culminates not in terror, but finally in humility
and reverential love. Though set in the harsh Canadian wilderness, this collection is more optimistic and affirmative than the
earlier *Flight into Darkness* which primarily depicts a wartime
urban environment. *Rocky Mountain Poems* does not ignore
danger or evil; the very first line of the book points out that cau-
tion is necessary—"There was a care needed"—while "Lake Hamil-
ton" alludes to the Fall, albeit humorously, making reference
to Lucifer, "forks and frying, and the thought of having been
up there."[26] The poems progress through laughter and love, however, culminating in flight—temporary transcendence. Mystery
remains, so that even in the final poem portions of the terrain remain unknown and unnamed; but the main feeling to emerge
is that

It
Was fine faring, finally, under
Ice, and green granting, the log
Latch giving, and fresh tea. (25)

At this point in his development, Gustafson highlights not what "Defeated us, muskeg, brush,/ Mosquitoes" (13), nor "death/dearest hurl" (23), but the cool, green, silent or thundering beauty of Canada's glaciers, peaks, forests, and falls.

III   Sift in an Hourglass

Sift in an Hourglass (1966) takes its title from Hopkins's *Wreck of the Deutschland,* a poem focussing on a contest between human beings and natural forces which results in terrifying, precipitous death. Although the Hopkins poem moves through the depiction of disaster—shipwreck in stormy seas—to a reaffirmation of Christian faith in the mastery of God, the lines that Gustafson isolates for his title come from an early section of the poem and speak only of the insecure, perilous, mortal condition, how we are like the sand or "sift" in an hourglass, doomed to run out in time. Unlike Hopkins's universe, Gustafson's is not even "at the wall/ Fast,"[27] for his is a world without the stability provided by religious faith and theological justification. Gustafson's typically anthropocentric vision is fully restored in this volume; he entitles one poem "Man Is the Creator Of." One draft of its opening lines runs: "It is man himself creates/ All things."[28] Consequently, there is no absolute but death; and, as Desmond Pacey noted in a contemporary review of *Sift in an Hourglass,* "in this latest book of poems, Ralph Gustafson is, like Webster, 'much possessed by death'."[29]

Gustafson's man centered theology and his ultimate values come more clearly into focus in *Sift in an Hourglass* than in any previous volume. In the fifty-seven poems of this collection, but most explicitly in the twelve poems of its opening section, death is a central reality; death and life are continually juxtaposed, and an Easter motif— the theme of resurrection, the cycles of birth and death—is ubiquitous. In ancient Semitic myths of creation, life and death were alternately victorious; and *Sift in an Hourglass* is close to the Old Testament notion that "to everything there is a season, and a time to every purpose. A time to be born, and a time to die."

"Aspects of Some Forsythia Branches," the opening poem, suggests the unity of all forms of life and the inevitability of these cyclical processes of generation and ruin. Cut from bushes which appear dead during winter, the forsythia branches are expected to flower, to "yellow" with bloom, in the spring. But the term "yellow" is ambiguous, for the "sear, the yellow leaf" in Shakespearean terms is symbolic of aging and death, and in Canadian terms yellow is a color of autumn. Gustafson himself records that "Somewhere death's in it"; as a result, flowerbeds become "deathbeds." The final lines are powerfully moving:

> So we cut branches two
> Days ago. Take great precautions.
> Go carefully through a door. Stand
> Among deathbeds as though among heroes,
> Pausing in winter along windy corridors
> With the knowledge ahead of us, to wrap our throats.[30]

The fragile, flowering shrubs which seem to contain within themselves the principle of their own renewal assume almost heroic proportions. The vulnerability of human life and its even greater dependencies are suggested by the defiant/pathetic gesture of looping a scarf around the neck against the bitter winds of winter, death.

Again in "The Exhortation," the second poem of the collection, winter and spring—death and life—are juxtaposed. It begins with a line thematically central to all Gustafson's adult poetry: "Grief's love's origin" (14). Roots and tubers which, like the forsythia branches of the previous poem, appear to be dry and lifeless are in fact "Taut with seed that in a burial/Springs." After one buries seed, it blossoms; the grave is thus a garden. Apparently in an effort to avoid the charge of willful obscurity levelled against his earlier work, Gustafson here glosses his own imagery.

> See,
> I'll unravel it: to plant a root
> You have to bury it. He who loses
> His life shall find it, etc., or,
> In rusted terms: we have to love. (14)

There are echoes of Christian dogma and the paradox that in order to save one's life one must lose it; also of John Donne, that each man's death diminishes us; and of Frost who in "Birches" insists that earth is still the right place for love. "The Exhortation" argues that

> what this asks is joy.
> Knowledge of sorrow is what I mean.
> By grief I mean joy. I talk
> To you flippantly in paradox.
> Understanding is lack of death. (15)

Gustafson's defiant attitude links him to the Anglo-Saxon poet of the *Battle of Maldon* ("Hige sceal pe heardra, heorte pe cenre,/ Mod sceal pe mare, pe ure maegen lytlaδ"), to Yeats ("and louder sing/ For every tatter in its mortal dress"), and to Auden ("We must love one another or die"). It also suggests that he is to be listed among Canadian writers such as Pratt, Smith, Layton, and Avison—all of whom express, in D. G. Jones's words, "a view of life that not only comprehends suffering and death but sees in them the conditions that make possible the highest human values."[31] In "The Silence," a poem from *Sift in an Hourglass* cited by Jones, Gustafson writes with a hushed, sober tone which marks a new departure after the wonder and affirmation of *Rocky Mountain Poems*: "All, all is sadness" (24). But responding to Pacey's critique that he is "much possessed by death," Gustafson maintains that "the whole book emphasizes death only to re-emphasize life."[32]

This paradox is explored in the poem "In a Quebec Field" which bears the transparent subtitle "An Accolade for Death who Makes Beauty Beauty." Garden imagery is again central, and there are puns on "undertakings" and "leavetakings"—the humor of punning itself one way of embodying Gustafson's rebellious response to mortality. "You've got him down/ that way./ Love" (22). Isolating the final word in a discrete line gives "Love" the force of an imperative, and indeed to love—not just Platonically but passionately—is Gustafson's one and only commandment.

His departures from orthodox Christianity are underscored further in poems such as "The Great Day," which mocks the idea of a literal resurrection of the body; "My Love Eats an Apple," which reverses the Genesis story and foreshadows the erotic/religious "Words for a Resurrection"; and "Fragment," a fantasy in which the persona imagines Christ's being revived from his martyr's posture to enjoy the beauty of the natural scene:

> Christ drew his arms in,
> And rubbed his drained wrists,
> And looked about him,
> Wondering at the holes his hands showed,
> The hill white with silver. (53)

Sift in an Hourglass, then, brings into focus several aspects of death: apparent death which leads to renewed life in seasonal succession; symbolic death in a quasiChristian context; and also literal death, the only creative issue of which is perhaps the poem itself.

In a poem such as "On the Exhumation of Anne Mowbray, Obiit Aged 9, 1481," the subject, as wellds as the Shaksperean diction, is retrieved from death and resurrected. Like Pound's *Cantos,* Gustafson's mature art brings to surface from underground not only buried subjects but also forgotten linguistic forms. Anne Mowbray, an obscure subject, was the child bride of one of the little princes murdered in fifteenth-century England in the Tower of London; she herself died or was murdered (the story is ambiguous) at the age of nine. Her coffin was exhumed in the 1960's; Gustafson describes her pitiful remains:

> Those hairs? A skull with tresses,
> Half a jaw—the other fallen.
> Look, a grin,
> A grin if you look right.
> Fugh! Away with it!
> Bury it, bury it
> Again,
> This maggot dripping flesh
> That sang and chewed on peppercorn
> And asked:
> To do to do to do in sheets. (19)

The graveyard scene in *Hamlet* and the language of this age itself are revived.

While the texture of *Rocky Mountain Poems* is like stone, that of *Sift in an Hourglass* is more like intricately woven tapestry. The interrelationships between structure and content in Gustafson's poetry offer an interesting area for critical exploration. When he writes of foreign countries or historical subjects or takes his inspiration from other works and forms of art, his writing tends to be allusive, complicated, elaborate; his "aboriginal" poetry, on the other hand, with its spare lyricism and stripped down description, is elicited almost exclusively by the Canadian terrain. "The Courtyard" and "And in that Winter Night" are revelatory in this context. The first is short enough to quote in full:

> The court
> Changes light.
> Between the backs of buildings
> Snow falls swiftly.
> The sills of windows
> Looking out on winter,
> The white pavements,
> Are without recall
> Or observance
> Or terror.
> Death
> Takes significance:
> Edmund the Prince called-to,
> Persepolis and all the helpless kings,
> Héloise
> Taking off her pale blue dress. (25)

The breathless, panicky lines underscore how snow falling in a Canadian winter night can assume the proportions of a vast, nonhuman force to which the only appropriate response appears to be submission. Death in a land where geography is more dominant than human traditions seems terrifying because so absolutely final. If any sense of human continuity is to be established, one must turn to older countries, foreign cultures. Here in the final lines Gustafson alludes to Edmund, the ninth-century king of the East Angles who was killed by invading Danes, and to Persepolis, the Persian capital sacked in the fourth century B.C. by Alexander the Great. The story of each man lives on: death seems less real, less final, in European contexts rich with legend, history, and art than in a newer country like Canada. But still, in either case, the ultimate response must be love. Héloise, celebrated for her defiant love of the medieval monk Peter Abelard, provides the poem's last image, a sexual one, "Taking off her pale blue dress."

"And in that Winter Night" develops further this central contrast between Europe (history) and Canada (geography). This poem juxtaposes two memories: one of a winter night in 1922 in Sherbrooke, Quebec, which is the subject also of Gustafson's story

"Snow"; the other of a visit in 1962 to the mausoleum of Empress Galla Placidia in Ravenna, Italy. Death may be contemplated in a European context within the manmade contours of a tomb decorated with mosaics which have outlasted centuries (Ravenna's mosaics conjured up thoughts of eternity in Yeats's "Sailing to Byzantium," too); but death assumes less manageable, indeed overwhelming, proportions in the open spaces of the Canadian landscape. No longer can the poet structure reality neatly as

> eight Beatitudes, Death
> the ninth, and crossed into four,
> north, south, east, west,
> the arch of the kingdom
> eternal. (34)

In the falling snow, dimensions scarcely exist; certainly reason cannot comprehend them. The poem continues in troubled, repetitive rhythms:

> the north broken with crystal,
> sleeve-broken, in winter,
> tumbling from that sky,
> myriad, the snow falling,
> light ineffable and death
> ineffable, the moment determining,
> understanding death, death
> understood under that winter night. (34–35)

By its structural parallelism, "And in that Winter Night" sets up an ostensible identity of the two experiences of death; but one is comprehensible in human terms (in the first section of the poem dealing with Europe, "Death" is personified), while the other appears to be uncontrollable and even incommunicable. Canada is no longer the cosy, hospitable country it was in "Quebec, Late Autumn" of *Rivers among Rocks*. In "Carta Canadensis" of *Sift in an Hourglass* Gustafson now projects his country as "rock eternal with loneliness" (31).

If section one of *Sift in an Hourglass* focusses primarily on death, section two, "Dramatis Personae," influenced by Browning's technique of dramatic monologue, highlights Gustafson's responses to death: typically these include love, joy, and defiant affirmation, but in the Canadian context, at times a feeling of total insignificance too.

That death is vulgar and comes to all is the common lesson repeated in "Ceremony," "Dirge for a Penny Whistle," and "For Arthur Smith and Irving Layton: As If They Were All Dead." But joy and dignity, as well as longevity in art, are nonetheless possible; this is apparent particularly in those poems in which Gustafson assumes the persona of another poet or artist.

The garden/grave motif presented in the opening poems is picked up again in "A Row of Geraniums." In fact, Linda Sandler has suggested that "gardening is a paradigm for life and poetry that's entirely [Ralph Gustafson's] own."[33] In a review of the later book *Fire on Stone*, Travis Lane conjectures that Gustafson's religion is "the concrete faith of the gardener . . . in spring-time."[34] Its affirmation in the face of death recalling "This Love is Not·a Praise" from *Rivers among Rocks*, "A Row of Geraniums" presents the musings of a gardener-persona who celebrates life because he is above ground at least:

> They say he is still alive who spades earth in a box,
> a row of geraniums
> laid out on the
> windowsill
> for the
> sun and the
> wind
> and the
> rain. . . . (42)

Rain symbolizes life, fertility, and hope. In fact, attitude is all important. As the volume's epigraph from Scarlatti suggests, one can increase pleasure and live happily by being more human than critical. Gustafson is never unaware of transience; but his chief emotional reaction, illogical as it may seem, involves deeper and deeper love.

This is the main theme again in "Concretions." The poem commemorates a day that Ralph and Betty Gustafson, together with Frank and Marian Scott (to whom *Sift in an Hourglass* is dedicated), went to Compton to hunt down the clay shapes a river can produce. Seeing "the cast/ Of the worm," the persona is moved to celebrate love.

> Through my love,
> Through my love,
> I invite the grass
> And dewy worm. (46)

"To My Love: Death's Pithy Paradox" imagines the figure of Death, limping on a crutch that is "bound with birth-/rags," as being jealous of "what we have,/True love/In bed and afterward." Love, sex, the phallic "green stick" are a mortal's only weapons against Death: "He comes quicker?/Cross him! Take/That green stick!" (47).

The most ambitious poem in the entire collection—in the whole Gustafson canon to date exclusive of the five long poems of *Theme and Variations for Sounding Brass*—is "Ariobarzanes." In it the destruction of Persepolis, seat of Persian civilization, is made to seem almost unimportant beside the individual lover's awareness of sexuality, natural beauty, and the varied sounds, sights, and smells of day-to-day living. This extended interior monologue in free verse records the convoluted patterns of thought and sense impression of a Macedonian youth, Ariobarzanes, who is one of two hundred Greeks hired to guard the first mistress of Darius III, king of Persia, just prior to the sack of his capital city by Alexander the Great in 330 B.C.

The poem opens with a structuring contrast between nature (the snow capped mountains) and civilization (Darius's opulent court). The decadence and artificiality of the court stand out: the major activities of the courtiers include watching peacocks and indulging in wine and sex. The situation between Ariobarzanes and the king's woman is depicted in a provocative vignette:

> he standing at her bronze door
> his weight taken on his hand on his lance
>   high up
> waiting guarding what? the nails of her feet
>   painted silver
> her hair undone and done up again
> her scrutiny
> her laugh her hand brushing the black under his
>   arm as she passed to the garden peacocks
>
> the black that was sweated. (54)

The opening section of the poem suggests both the tumescence of Ariobarzanes and his speculative nature as he reflects on his life from a cool mountain perch.

The second section of the poem carries the initial oppositions to a more comprehensive and philosophical level, while simultaneously bringing them into sharper focus. The main antinomies are intellect and passion; they are symbolized by two different Persian cities, Istachr—which adjoined Persepolis and was a center of priestly learning—and the decadent Persepolis itself. In other terms the antagonism is between Circe and moly, carnal indulgence and restraint (moly being the herb given Odysseus by Hermes against the spell of the enchantress). The intellect is "clean/cold in thought"; by contrast, sensuality and sexual passion are repeatedly depicted in terms of sweat, heat, and light: "Helios! Helene! Troy burned in that light!" (56). More basically, the choice is between life ("Light light!") and death ("the clipped yew/the lugubrious tree"). In several respects "Ariobarzanes" of *Sift in an Hourglass* is a companion piece for "All That Is in the World" from *Rivers among Rocks,* although the emphases are reversed: in "Ariobarzanes" the temptations to sexual indulgence are excessive and culminate in destruction, whereas in "All That Is in the World" puritanical injunctions for sexual repression run to extremes and are life negating. Alexander the Great, educated by Aristotle whose philosophy emphasizes moderation, is victorious here; and the youthful Ariobarzanes, fleeing the decadent city, lives on to enjoy the wholesome beauties of sea and mountains, as well as private sexual delights with a peasant girl he encounters.

Section three of the poem contains the essence of Gustafson's wisdom: his answer to death is in acclaimed sensuality. He records that "the summer roses sustained answers" (57). Not the jealous, coy, painted eroticism of Darius's court, but rather unashamed natural beauty is what he celebrates. This portion of the poem can also be read as an almost allegorical statement about art itself since it alludes to the defeat of Bellerophon who failed in his attempt to ride the winged steed Pegasus—symbol of poetic inspiration—to heaven. It seems noteworthy not only that Ariobarzanes opts for sensuality ("he'd screw Helen") over intellect ("Why strain in the Academy?"), but that Gustafson also chooses a sensuous style rather than the more intellectual one of poems such as those opening *Rivers among Rocks,* for instance. His artistry thus reinforces the vision of life which the poem expresses.

> There is a pledge of death in all things
> yet he turned from himself knowing,
> the market place having no less the big answers
> the bronze-monger at the stall
> the white bulls
> the horsesmith's hide apron
> the crowd standard for Friday mornings
> the celery wilting and the oranges
> the iron scales hanging,
> as men are aware of such things. (57)

Sensuality and sexuality both are touchstones: "the coriander was the big answers/the white seed of the coriander" (58).

Section four, switching to the first person pronoun, traces the fall of Persepolis; section five, Ariobarzanes' journey, both physical and psychological. Darius's tragedy suggests the transience of all life— "the jaw broken that had sucked the honey/the sculptured jaw in the dung" (60); but only as an afterthought does Ariobarzanes mention an other-worldly ceremony of recognition ("Tomorrow I shall sail to Scios/sacrificing three doves" [62]). His primary response to mutability and disintegration is to regale himself upon the beauty of the sea- and mountainscapes. His impassioned, cinematic survey of the natural scene is recreated in highly sensuous language, tempting the sight with colors of green, gold, and white; the smell with odors of citron, hyacinth, and leather; the taste with fruits and spices such as coriander and saffron; the touch with the texture of hair, snow, and marble; the hearing with seductive patterns of sound, repetitions, and onomatopoeic descriptions.

> the sands were gold
>   sucking in seafoam
> the laced sands
> as I rode high on the cliffs
>   the stallion
> the sidling cream stallion
>   snuffing
> the air salt and the musk
> my thighs pressed
> on the white apron of the harness
>   citron on leather
> . . . .
> the wind strong on the cliff
>   and the white foam below
> the towers of Persepolis burning
> red in the afterglow. (60)

One of the main characteristics of Gustafson's mature poetry is this ability to structure words in patterns so that the sound echoes the sense. His current reputation as an expert craftsman is based principally on this skill in weaving the verbal texture of his poems. The medium highlights the message.

Moving from death to love, *Sift in an Hourglass* ends by focussing on art, as if art were the ultimate strategy for staving off annihilation. But the third and final section of this collection, subtitled "The Year of Voyages," which recreates the experience of Gustafson's trip to Europe in the summer of 1962, is the weakest in the book. Surveying a variety of European monuments, museums, cathedrals, and so on, several of the poems are mere travel diary jottings. Gustafson attempts to create art from art—from literature, paintings, concerts, dramatic performances, illuminations, architecture, mosaics, sculptures, and frescoes. But some of these art poems do not move from fact into significance, from object to symbol, from the personal to the universal; they fail to break out of the circle of Gustafson's own private associations. Noticing a little lamb in mosaics ("The Procession of Virgins: Sant' Apollinare Nuovo: Ravenna") and a black eye on a lithograph of Pan ("On Seeing in a Gothenburg Art Gallery on a Picasso a Blackeye") are two trivial personal observations which communicate nothing of significance.

There are, however, some committed and vital poems among the weaker ones. "On the Top of Milan Cathedral" is a convincing satirical portrait of contemporary consumer society. The Browningesque "Galla Placidia, Empress of the West, Builds Her Tomb: Ravenna" is a skillful interior monologue in the third person which delicately juxtaposes love and death. The Yeatsian "Swans of Vadstena," a love poem recapitulating some of the themes of "Ariobarzanes," underscores the healing power of love:

> She turns from the violence
> To my violence, taken in the white
> Tumult, unbelieving, making known
> And whole the blemished god. (85)

The best ever of Gustafson's poems imitative of Anglo-Saxon verse is "At Durham"; its theme—courage in the face of death—is central to both his own and Old English poetry. "At Will Shakespeare's Grave" again juxtaposes love and death, and the last word is love. Like the best of *Rivers among Rocks,* the best of *Sift in an Hourglass* is quintessentially Gustafson "original." The book as a whole is a *momento mori,* like the final poem referring to William Blake; and the collection underscores the Blakean wisdom that eternity is in love with the productions of time.

IV Ixion's Wheel

Ralph Gustafson's *Ixion's Wheel* (1969), like Irving Layton's *The Whole Bloody Bird* published the same year, results from world travel and mature reflection on the meaning of life. As one reviewer stated suggestively, *Ixion's Wheel* offers a "contemporary Grand Tour of no-longer-innocents among the ruins."[35] Reprinting *Rocky Mountain Poems* and all but six of the poems of "The Year of Voyages" from *Sift in an Hourglass,* the collection also presents fifty-four new poems composed during two trips in 1965 and 1967 to Britain, Western and Eastern Europe, and the Middle East. Throughout the book, as D. G. Jones pointed out in his review for *Canadian Literature,* the poetry focusses on "human desire in revolt against banality and death."[36]

The concluding lines of one of Layton's world tour poems, a poem inspired by the Taj Mahal, register that "beauty lies/in the perfect symmetry/of death and Eros."[37] Love and death are equally central to Gustafson's vision, as a poem like "At the Trevi Fountain: Rome" graphically illustrates. This thematically key poem is a pithy reflection on the celebrated statue of Oceanus (oldest of the children of Uranus and Gaea, the Titans who constituted the first race) standing, as it does in the Roman fountain, between Death on one side and Fertility on the other. By association, the Trevi Fountain calls to the poet's mind the water of Hippocrene, gushing azure water—struck from the ground by Pegasus—which conferred poetic inspiration on those who drank of it. Gustafson's poem thus not only directs attention to the twin realities of copulation and dying, but also posits these twin realities as the source of art.

Greek mythology figures prominently in *Ixion's Wheel,* a volume taking its title from one of the more notorious lovers of classical antiquity. According to myth, Ixion, king of the Lapithae, while engaged to marry Dia, daughter of Eioneus, had a dispute with his future father-in-law and killed him. After this crime, Ixion sought refuge with Zeus on Mount Olympus; dining with the gods, Ixion turned his eyes towards Zeus's exquisitely beautiful wife Hera and was inflamed with irresistible desire. In the madness of his passion, Ixion even embraced a cloud which Zeus had shaped to resemble Hera. Ixion, chastized for his insolence, was bound in Hades to a fiery, perpetually turning wheel. Gustafson's title, then, refers to unquenchable sexual passion, but also, by extension through the epigraph taken from Pound's "Canto 113," to ceaseless intellectual desire as well. In fact where *Ixion's Wheel* differs significantly from *The Whole Bloody Bird* is in its more allusive, impersonal, metaphysical drive. Gustafson's learning and intellectual sophistication are distinctive; after reading this 1969 volume, A. J. M. Smith—a highly metaphysical poet himself, of course—wrote in a personal letter to Ralph Gustafson that *Ixion's Wheel* demonstrates that Gustafson is "the most learned and allusive poet in Canada."[38]

In his travel poems, Gustafson attempts to move beyond a mere recital of fact towards an illumination of value and significances on a universal plane. What Gustafson searches for, as he records in "The Philosophy of the Parthenon," is "The truth, not as an existence / But as a meaning."[39] Recreating his visits to art museums, graves of earlier artists, famous ruins of past civilizations, or infamous landmarks of the twentieth century (such as Dachau), Gustafson tries—as Mallarmé had urged—to paint not the thing but the effect it produces. A few uncommuted poems, however, betray an over-concern with formal elements of poetry such as rhythm and sound, turning one of the main distinguishing features of his work into merely a superficial end in itself. There is a lack of vitality and direction in some poems. In his review for the *Montreal Star,* Bryan McCarthy rightly complained that there is "a lifeless quality reminiscent of a heap of fragmented statuary."[40] But increasingly as Gustafson moves from the "Second Year" section to the "Third Year," there is a livelier sense of visceral response and commitment. The opening lines of "Kammer Konzert, Neue Schloss, Bayreuth" seem nearly self-parodic: "Form. Form" (112). The specter of sterile formalism, form without content, hovers over such poems as "Marble Fragment: British Museum," "Kandinsky: Improvisation No. 26," or "La Chute d'Icare." But the strong, stately rhythms which carry "The Valley of Kings" or "At a Performance of Euripides' *The Trojan Women*: Epidaurus" are effective and indeed striking.

The influence of music on Gustafson's writing is noteworthy in *Ixion's Wheel* not only in the crafted rhythms and sounds of his lines; music itself becomes the subject of several poems. Three are written about modern Hungarian composer and pianist Franz Liszt. In "Franz Liszt: Tivoli" Gustafson presents a very personal imaginary portrait of Liszt at Villa d'Este as an old man in carpet slippers poised, like Oceanus, between death—the black cypresses—and life—water threaded with bird song. Gustafson's persona himself is placed in this ambiguous position in "At Franz Liszt's Grave" as he stands between the musician's gravestone and his own loved one who is "Listening for the bird" (91). The third Liszt poem is inspired by the sight of his *stümmflugel,* his dummy piano. "Franz Liszt's Dummy Piano: Bayreuth" wrestles with the Idealist/ Nominalist dilemma. Gustafson rejects the Ideal, "Solemn transcension, / The Heavenly

Bridegroom," and, unlike poets from *Pearl* to *Paradise Lost,* affirms
the here and now:

> What matter,
> The heavenly angle—
>
> . . . .
> In the mind is Paradise
> And here the wangled
> Consummation. (92)

Another three poem series centers on Shakespeare: "At Will's
Grave Again," "To Will Shakespeare, Gent.," and "For the Third
Time (with My Love) Some Doggerel for Will." In the first poem,
despite the inescapable knowledge that "death's above/all of us,"
Gustafson reiterates that love between mortal man and woman is
supremely valuable. Anne Shakespeare and Betty Gustafson both
figure in "At Will's Grave Again," which judges: "you'd fooled death
anyway,/the way you lived" (94).

Like Auden's "Petition," Gustafson's fourteen-line "To Will Shakespeare, Gent." begins formally with the persona's humbly addressing
the greater man as "Sir" and offering a report of the state of society.
In short, "The world is worse" than in Shakespeare's age. Echoing
Yeats's "The Second Coming," Gustafson's poem tells of "ceremony
lost" and "The best indifferent." Wrily, the persona recommends
Shakespeare to "Keep/To your grave"; but paradoxically he also
asserts of the world: "Love of it our credentials" (120). In Gustafson's
vision, as in Auden's, the historical world, though fallen, is redeem-
able through love.

"For the Third Time (with My Love) Some Doggerel for Will"
searches for a definition of the role of the poet in this botched
civilization, these "coarse times." In the last line, the poet is labelled a
"Disturber of good sound minds" (120). This definition provides a
logical base for the fully *engagé* poems of Gustafson's next collection,
Theme and Variations for Sounding Brass. Moreover, in *Ixion's
Wheel* itself Gustafson does not withdraw from death, distortion, and
destruction. His quest through the museums of Europe and the
monuments of the ancient civilizations of the Mediterranean and the
Nile constitutes less an escape from the present than an Odyssean
voyage through the underworld of history to find out what is still of
relevance.

In the relics of the pagan civilizations of Greece and Egypt, Gustafson finds more meaning than in Christian art work and cathedrals.

The antisex bias of Christianity is attacked in "The Mosaics, Kariye Djami: Istanbul" as Joseph, the pragmatic carpenter, is depicted doubting the possibility of a virgin birth. A still more explicit denunciation of Christian dogma is given in "The Resurrection of the Body: Morning Prayer, Westminster Abbey." But amidst the mummies and pyramids of the Nile, Gustafson discovers evidence of a religion which comes close in its orientation to his own emphasis on sensuality. "The Valley of Kings" begins: "They weren't far wrong:/the body kept/to keep the soul" (70). Coming on the jewelry of the Egyptian princess Khnoumit preserved in the Cairo Museum, he poses the question without answer: "What heaven/Equals Nefertiti?" (69). His values are not dissimilar to those of fertility cults with gods such as "Menn of the thrusting thigh" (68) and "That bearded phallus, Zeus" (75). In a humorous vein, the persona of "A Conviction: Not far off Salamis" reflects on the stories of Uranus, Leda, and Orithyia to justify his conclusion that coition is divine. Finally in "The Histiaean Poseidon: Athens," looking at the fifth-century B.C. bronze statue of the Greek god of the sea (whose love affairs were almost as numerous if less celebrated than those of Zeus), the Christianized persona is moved to a passionate identification with the primitive divinity:

> I cry blasphemy.
> Cry,
> The hurl of the god
> Is my hurl. (77)

Death, of course, cannot be conquered totally even by love. This is brought home emphatically by the powerfully concise "Old Lady Seen Briefly at Patras." Gustafson is both empathetic and ironic as he juxtaposes the image of an old woman hobbling along on a cane with the goddess of love:

> The stick firm, a short
> Crosspiece on top, each side
> The hands control the gift of earth
> To walk back to her door.
> Sixty years back she lay naked
> To be loved, thighs the width of him.
> But the walk is on cobbles,
> Not too good at best, not
> With bent spine and incontinence.

> Aphrodite's laugh was certain
> (These are reliable reports),
> Not too loud; derisive, but lovely. (116)

The poem combines a bitterness that time transfigures woman with a note of tragic gaiety: myth and art live on. A similarly defiant poem "On the Bull-leapers' Fresco: Knossos" concludes: "Than the assault, the danger is/to love the last time" (73).

Gustafson persistently celebrates "this testament of drenching/ Love, such as it is" even if only "For the moment the testimony of the actual; earth breaking/In colour." Not just individual aging and death, but collective dying and destruction (Dachau, Vietnam) are mentioned, too, in "Am Bachsee, with Thoughts of Vietnam" in which these lines occur. This poem juxtaposes alpine beauty with the hideousness of war and notes—as if to register the fact for the future poems of *Theme and Variations for Sounding Brass*—"Violence is sometimes/Too quick for the wound to be immediately determined./ But it will be"/ (109).

One of the finest poems in *Ixion's Wheel* is "At the Pinakothek Ruins: Munich" which deals with the West's destructive bent from the Renaissance through to the mid twentieth century—from Savonarola's burning to the bombing of London. Savonarola was the leader of the religious reaction against the artistic licence of the Renaissance. Gustafson regards his attitude as life negating and, as such, analogous to warfare which also destroys "all man's good things." Restricted by religious negations here symbolized by the cowl—a monk's hooded garment—human beings are throttled back in a self-destructive way. The poem concludes: "Man bears just so much ecstasy,/And thunders in his cowl." The antilife influence of the Christian church is attacked once again, as Gustafson, poet, places himself on the side of transient beauty, "Beauty out of flesh,/ Out of dust, perfection" (89). Gustafson provides his own gloss for this poem in his whimsical notes at the end of the collection. "I am not much for burning anybody, even Savonarola whom the Florentines finally set alight, fed up with his fulminations against nudity, jewels, poems, songs, girls, and other unnecessary things; but one must oppose man's inability to sustain the arts" (123).

The poem which concludes the "Third Year" section is "Among the Elgin Marbles." It ends with a prayer for peace which bears striking resemblance to portions of *Alfred the Great* written some thirty years earlier. Gustafson reiterates his longing for peace, love, and fruitfulness.

Daughter of Zeus,
grant peace.
That the slim-thighed youths have maidens,
that the corn ripen,
the olive,
and that women, weeping,
no longer mourn. (99)

The best poem of *Ixion's Wheel* and one of the finest of Gustafson's entire career is "Agamemnon's Mask: Archeological Museum, Athens." It is an art poem inspired by the gold death mask of an Achaean king which was found by the nineteenth-century archeologist Heinrich Schliemann in one of the royal tombs on the Acropolis of Mycenae and initially thought to be that of Agamemnon, commander of the Greek forces in the Trojan War, though later dated to a much earlier period. Like Keats's Grecian urn, this artifact inspires in the poet quiet reflections on the universal cycles of birth, copulation, and death.

Flattened, beaten out,
The mask of gold.
But an earlier king, they say,
Miscalled by Schliemann
Digging around, over-anxious,
His mind on windy Troy
And that return to Argos'
Scented bath—
Some Achaean king,
Loved, I suppose,
Who also had children,
Was important,
As the rest of us,
Eating the red bean,
Digesting the day,
Without legend,
Praying the gods,
Without much hope,
Then dying:
The gravesmith,
Out of love,
Beating the fine gold,
The drained face laid away,
Without much trouble,
Without complication,
Without much trouble to anyone.
No matter.
Let it be Agamemnon's. (78)

Gustafson's simplified, almost prosy language and plain rhythms, which were first perfected to depict the Canadian Rockies, here shape an elegy which, like the gold death mask, fits many men. Gustafson's two separate styles—one direct, the other allusive—hitherto elicited by two distinct orders of experience (one involving Canadian nature and weather, and the other, European art and myth), which have been conveyed by two different types of imagery—one geographical, the other historical—begin by the end of the 1960's to merge.

CHAPTER 6

Poetry of the 1970's: Tracks in the Snow

THE full depth and range of Ralph Gustafson's mature work become apparent with the four collections of his poetry published during the 1970's: *Selected Poems* (1972), *Theme and Variations for Sounding Brass* (1972), *Fire on Stone* (1974), and *Corners in the Glass* (1977). During this fertile period, too, critical neglect of Gustafson's poetry ended abruptly with his winning of two important awards: in 1975 *Fire on Stone* was distinguished with both the A. J. M. Smith Award for Poetry from Michigan State University and the coveted Canadian Governor General's Literary Award.

Publication of a volume of selected poems is usually a sign that a poet is reviewing his work and moving on. For Ralph Gustafson around the turn of the decade, this is clearly the case. In 1972, the same year McClelland and Stewart published his *Selected Poems,* Gustafson privately brought out a small pamphlet of strikingly different poems which commercial publishing houses in Canada would not touch—the politically committed poems of *Theme and Variations for Sounding Brass.* Gustafson designed his own covers for both collections, and a comparison of the two is instructive about the nature of the change then coming over his art. The dustjacket of *Selected Poems* shows a reproduction of a smashed jasper bust of Queen Tiye, which dates back to around 1380 B.C. This ancient, fragmented, Egyptian head of a once beautiful woman, carved in the hardest material after diamond, is a resonant example of the image of the skull which recurs so often in Gustafson's poems; it epitomizes simultaneously the transient nature of everything belonging to this sublunary universe—even the beautiful and the loved—and also, paradoxically, the longevity of art.

Poles apart is the cover design of *Theme and Variations for Sounding Brass.* This is a collage of recent newspaper headlines and journalistic photographs of current political events—including a Soviet tank wreaking destruction in Czechoslovakia, the carnage of a Quebec mailbox bombing, and clippings about the destitution of millions of Bangladesh refugees. The first design is aesthetic, individualistic, and static; the second design, political, collective, and dynamic. These contrasting images are indicative of a dramatic redirection in Gustafson's writing; as he explains, "I got sick of hearing that I'm a romantic who writes about the head of Nefertiti."[1]

His new witness literature, then, is the product of a deliberate decision to deal directly in poetry with the international political brutalities and injustices of the late 1960's and early 1970's. But still, even in this witness literature, the overriding theme is love, not just on an individual level but on a broader social and political one. Throughout his career, Gustafson is saying "we must love one another or die, as Auden said."[2] The thematic unity of his mature poetry is impressive. Although Fred Cogswell once dismissed the thematic aspect of Gustafson's work as "essentially a simple, uncomplicated response to experience" and an attitude which "seldom goes beyond praise of beauty and decency and revulsion against their opposites,"[3] a closer examination reveals that, on the contrary, Gustafson's philosophy is richly inclusive, yoking together the major antinomies of time and eternity, brevity and beauty, nature and art, life and death, and good and evil. In his review of *Selected Poems,* Christopher Xerxes Ringrose speaks suggestively of Gustafson's pervasive "sense of the mysterious co-presence of life and death in the world, in the imagination, in art, an equipoise tilting delicately towards the grave."[4]

Notwithstanding their high degree of thematic unity, however, Gustafson's poems exhibit a wide diversity of form, tone, style, and imagery. Just in the new collections of the 1970's alone, structures range from the mixed media protest poems of *Theme and Variations for Sounding Brass* articulated in bold, plain, proselike statements, through the subtlety and allusiveness of the meditative *Fire on Stone,* to the personal lyric epiphanies of *Corners in the Glass.* His technical virtuosity has quite rightly earned him a reputation for masterly craftsmanship, while the redirection of his art in recent years has provided an unusual example of what Doug Fetherling has termed a poet "growing younger, in outlook and method"[5] as the Modern and postModern parts of Gustafson's sensibility have come increasingly to dominate the traditional part. The process of updating began back in the mid 1930's, but it is given renewed emphasis in the 1970's. As a result, Gustafson's winning of the Governor General's Literary Award for 1974 signifies more than just belated recognition of a fine poet. Over the years Gustafson has been consciously striving to be more immediate, less elliptical, less difficult. Finding an audience, he has with greater consistency written poems that are not only magnificent verbal structures but, as Sandler was among the first to note, the speech acts of a man powerfully and persuasively communicating with his readers as well.

I Selected Poems

As a means of summing up the main lines of Gustafson's poetic development up to the 1970's, it is useful to consider very briefly his *Selected Poems* of 1972. Although his revisions for this book are neither numerous nor extensive, his choices of poems for inclusion or omission are significant for assessing his attitude to his own work, as well as his present critical tastes and general philosophical values. As may be anticipated, not a single verse from his first two books—*The Golden Chalice* and *Alfred the Great*—is included in *Selected Poems*. Nevertheless, although Gustafson dissociates himself completely from his early, introverted, imitative, Romantic style, his affirmative attitude which celebrates the world even while judging it, his imaginative identification with nature, and his penchant for the lyric mode remain basic constants.

Of the poems written during his transitional phase from the mid 1930's to the mid 1940's, Gustafson includes twenty. His choices range widely to present a few traditional sonnets, as well as the Hopkinsian "Mythos," the Spanish Civil War poem "Basque Lover," and the MacNeicean "April Eclogue"—a poem which marks the first really major turning point in his writing career. These transitional poems represent an important step in the modernization of Gustafson's poetic style; but in themselves, for the most part, they are very imperfect assimilations of the techniques of Gustafson's models at the time: Hopkins, Eliot, MacNeice, Auden, and Spender.

Selected Poems presents chiefly poetry Gustafson has written since the mid 1940's. It includes twenty-six poems from each of *Rivers among Rocks* and *Sift in an Hourglass,* all but four of *Rocky Mountain Poems,* and thirty-three of the poems collected for the first time in *Ixion's Wheel.* In all there are 119 poems chosen from Gustafson's books between 1944 and 1969, as well as two previously uncollected ones: "Where a Poem Departs from the Truth"—the opening poem which provides Gustafson's current aesthetic values and underscores the role of the poet as a moral agent—and "For Arthur Smith"—which seems to invite a direct comparison of Gustafson and Smith, and acknowledge recognition of a shared concern for fastidious craftsmanship. These selected poems range in tone from ebullient wittiness to open passion (in the love lyrics), or from moral indignation and satire to macabre jocularity and irony (in the poetic resuscitations of the highly successful dramatic monologues). But the overriding mood is passionate defiance. In a perceptive comment on *Fire on Stone,* which can be applied much more widely, Sandler has noted that Gustafson characteristically tends to "show man as a sort of passionate stone condemned to death—who nevertheless defies death by loving, suffering, thinking and making art."[6]

The arrangement of *Selected Poems* is not chronological, but rather thematic, which highlights this position. The collection builds from a double foundation of poems about poetry ("Prefatory") and about the poet himself ("Biography"). The third section, "On This Sea-Floor," documents Gustafson's quarrel with Christianity; the fourth, "Gothic Fugue," his quarrel with the destructive tendencies of this age; and the fifth, "Rivers among Rocks," his quarrel with death itself. Affirmation of the supreme value of love between man and woman constitutes the impressive central section, "Armorial"; this is followed by celebration and exploration of the beauty and harshness of nature, especially Canadian nature ("Of Place" and "Rocky Mountain Poems"). The penultimate section, "Portraits," groups together various short dramatic monologues, underscoring Gustafson's increasingly direct ties to Ezra Pound and emphasizing personality, zest, and dignity. Finally his poems suggestively reach into "Music and Imagery," with the very last poem—the highly sensuous and mellifluous "Ariobarzanes"—offering a passionate meditation on the tripleheaded divinity of Gustafson's secular religion: sex, nature, and death.

The inclusiveness of Gustafson's vision embraces those three major subjects, as well as art and myth. Many of his *Selected Poems*—almost all of those chosen from *Ixion's Wheel,* for example—deal with European history and art, or classical history and myth. But Gustafson's grappling with the unjustifiable fact of death in his nature poems, particularly relevant in terms of the Canadian experience, yields fresh and interesting insights. The question of Canadian cultural identity—raised also in Gustafson's anthologies of Canadian prose and poetry—is given poetic statement primarily in the two "aboriginal" sections subtitled "Of Place" and "Rocky Mountain Poems." What emerges from these nature poems chiefly is a realization of how the alien beauty of this cold northern land presents striking objective correlatives for the state of mind of a man confronting his own mortality. Gustafson maps Canada as an "iron land"; over "rock eternal with loneliness"[7] the snow falling in a winter night can assume the proportions of a vast, nonhuman, dictatorial force which reduces the significance of human achievement to near nothingness.

When the setting is the Quebec townships, Gustafson's attitude is more fully affirmative, however, with a sense of his being at peace and at home. The contrast between the rest of the war torn world and the rural calm of the townships emerges as another innovative, recurring motif—at least in those poems written prior to the wave of separatist terrorism in Quebec which in 1970 culminated with political kidnapping and murder (a subject he treats later in "Aubade: Quebec"). His ultimate response to the terrain of Canada thus stresses reverential love for its magnificence but also incorporates feelings of loneness, incomprehension, and even powerlessness before the overwhelming strength of the forces of nature. Generalizing from personal experience, Gustafson once explained to an Australian radio audience that "despite our cold Yukon, notice, too, that despite all our groanings and driftings, we really love our winter and its solitude. Lampman in the 1890's was loving it. Like Robert Frost having to make up his mind in a New England winter, the Canadian in the Eastern Townships where I live only thirty miles from the Vermont border, he too has to make terrible decisions. But not all the time. Sometimes our winters are as cosy as a Quebec stove."[8]

Possibly this different attitude to nature in the townships arises because parts of this region, unlike much of Canada, afford rounded and limited perspectives—not totally unlike those of the English Lake District—where the human figure is less of an anomaly. Or perhaps it is because this quiet and pastoral terrain is associated with his childhood that the region around Lake Massawippi often functions in Gustafson's poetry as a symbol of peace and innocence. Of course, no absolute contrast and separation between Europe and Canada is possible; that European wars have always had repercussions here Gustafson noted as early as "Crisis" written in 1938. Nor are the townships immune to the ravages of time, technology, pollution, political violence, and man's inhumanity. In fact, around 1970 Gustafson's Quebec poems begin to suggest that now people have taken up the powers of senseless destruction previously ascribed only to the wilderness.

II   Theme and Variations for Sounding Brass

Love, the central imperative of Ralph Gustafson's writing from first to last, is extended as the one redeeming and indispensable social virtue in the protest poems of *Theme and Variations for Sounding Brass* (1972). Dedicated to the victims of international violence and political injustice from Quebec and Ohio to Russia, Czechoslovakia, Greece, Biafra, Vietnam, Cambodia, and Bangladesh, this collection of five long poems takes its title from I Corinthians: "Though I speak with the tongues of men and of angels, and have not charity, I am become as sounding brass, or a tinkling cymbal" (13:1). In the biblical hymn, love or charity is praised as superior to knowledge, thaumaturgy, martyrdom, faith, and hope; as exhibiting all the other virtues combined; and as never failing. But the tragedy to which Gustafson penetrates is that, in a world increasingly inured to the horrors of brutal military and political events rehearsed almost daily in the news media, love can ultimately fail; there is, in the end, "too/ Much death for compassion."[9] As a result, the poet has a special task to "Shock our hearts" (poem 4), to restore our numbed sensibilities, and to prevent us from evading the extent and significance of these grotesque and inhuman contemporary realities. Thus, like Pound whom he has come to regard as "the most stimulating man of our century,"[10] Gustafson in *Theme and Variations for Sounding Brass* makes a heroic endeavor to communicate with a blockhead epoch.

The collective structure which contains the five poems—theme and variations—is borrowed from music, as are each of the five individual structures: nocturne, fantasia, ricercare, aubade, and coda. The theme at the heart of the volume is love; and the variations show, in a range of international contexts, the grim, dehumanizing results of its distortion or ultimate absence. No other Canadian poet equals Gustafson's intensity and range in rounding on the horrors of international violence—not even the militant Milton Acorn, younger poet John Baglow, or Irving Layton who is dedicated to writing poems that will "rip your skin off." Three of the five poems of *Theme and Variations for Sounding Brass* were staged as highly successful mixed media presentations in the early 1970's. "Nocturne: Prague 1968," with a musical score by British composer Richard Arnell, Professor of Composition at Trinity College of Music, given its premiere at Bishop's University in March 1970, drew a standing ovation from the capacity audience. Gustafson narrated the poem, while Arnell at the piano directed a choral group and rock band in coordination with a tape of electronic music and film clips of the invasion of Czechoslovakia. Subsequently, this poem was presented at the Arts Festival of Hofstra University in New York and was broadcast by the C.B.C. on the program "Anthology." The C.B.C. then commissioned two further mixed media presentations, one for radio and the other for television. The first became Gustafson's "Coda: I Think of All Soft Limbs" and was scored by Arnell for a singer commentating on the poem as read by Gustafson and accompanied by Arnell on piano, with electronic music composed by Tristram Cary. The second became "Ricercare: And Still These Deaths Are Ours," a poem written to rivet the television viewer's eyes on pictures of Bangladesh war victims and refugees. The poem and pictures were broadcast on the program "Viewpoint" which immediately follows the national evening news.

In personal correspondence, Richard Arnell confided to Gustafson: "Your poetry appeals to everyone, but I think your political poems really hit the students as few of our generation's poets seem to do—the way in fact that Auden and Spender hit me as a schoolboy."[11] Doug Fetherling called the collection "the best work he has done to date," and George Jonas wrote: "It puts contemporary events in the perspective of more lasting ideas and ideals."[12] *Theme and Variations for Sounding Brass* clearly expands the range of Gustafson's work, but it is not an entirely new departure, having had precedents in earlier volumes. *Flight into Darkness* from 1944, for example, contains a number of topical and committed poems: "Basque Lover," written against the background of the Spanish Civil War; "On the Struma Massacre," inspired by the plight of Jewish refugees during World War II; and the poems of "Sequence to War" which reflect the uneasy 1930's drift to global confrontation in a form less veiled than the political allegory of *Alfred the Great*. Gustafson's postwar stories, too, demonstrate his capacity to deal with violence, sadism, and psychological trauma. The 1972 collection, therefore, actually represents the poetic culmination of his facing up to political events, while the bold rhetorical devices and mixed media arrangements he utilizes here for the first time bring this previously submerged aspect of his writing to wide public attention.

In one of these witness poems, "Fantasia on Four Deaths," Gustafson writes:

> I slip
> From parable, sarcastic wit,
> Didactics O to plain
> Statement! (poem 2)

This assessment, by and large, is an accurate summary of the major change in his style. It grows noticeably simpler and more direct; his language moves closer to prose in terms of vocabulary, syntax, and rhythm. In fact, in some instances, patterns of reference are established by means of incorporating into the poetry snatches of prose, usually from political speeches. This is seen first in "Nocturne: Prague 1968" and becomes the main structuring principle of "Fantasia on Four Deaths," which is virtually a found poem. There is a very interesting connection, then, between Gustafson's response to the Rockies and to the political events of the 1960's. In both cases he encounters realities for which parable and metaphor seem irrelevant. In *Rocky Mountain Poems* he refers to the overwhelming grandeur of nature; in *Theme and Variations for Sounding Brass* he writes of historical forces and of "too/Much death" (poem 5). For both experiences, it seems, only "plain/Statement" suffices.

1. *"Nocturne"*

The nocturne (literally, "night music") by definition is a quiet, reflective, slow piece of music—although in Chopin its usual mood of meditative, gentle elegy may be broken by contrasting sections of a passionate nature. It is this episodic modern form which Gustafson uses as his structural model for "Nocturne: Prague 1968," a poem about the Russian led Warsaw Pact invasion of Czechoslovakia on the night of 20–21 August 1968 which terminated Alexander Dubcek's eight-month experiment in liberalising Communism. Written in twenty-one short verse paragraphs, this poem begins and ends in a peaceful, pastoral setting (first in Franconia, then Quebec). The tranquil rural scene—cool green fields, sun, flowers—provides a contrast with the central urban setting of steel tanks, turrets, lampposts, and garbage pails. While the theme of betrayal implicit from the opening paragraphs recalls *Alfred the Great,* the juxtaposition of nature and artillery in "Nocturne" is reminiscent of *Epithalamium in Time of War.* But Gustafson's mood here does not reach into jubilation; his persona remains achingly somber.

> What is it possible to propose
> against tanks, against armour
> on the roads, in the streets of Czechoslovakia?
> Green fields? September?
> . . . .
> There is no known weapon to counter tanks.

The poem was well researched in popular news sources including *Time, Life, Newsweek,* the *New York Times,* the *New Statesman,* and the *Montreal Star.*[13] Not just the major event of invasion, but background political material such as the Cierna summit and even small details of individual behavior can be documented in these sources: the Soviet tanks' hitting Bratislava, Slovakia's capital, at such speed that they knocked down lampposts; Czech youths' dumping of garbage on the hot tanks to create a stench—a token of the remarkable Czech campaign of passive resistance; or the picture of a miniskirted girl pushing a baby stroller during what journalists termed the country's "springtime of freedom." In fact, parts of the poem—such as the citations from President Ludvik Svoboda or from the unnamed announcer on a free radio station—are taken verbatim from news sources.

This closeness to news sources perhaps accounts for the prosy nature of certain passages. The ninth verse paragraph, for example, reads:

> The streets were taken in a night.
> Despite the fact that it was unexpected
> it was incredibly efficient.
> The mild and ideologically quiet Dubcek
> was in manacles by morning.

This is poetry at the opposite extreme from the elliptical, contorted, Hopkinsian language found in *Rivers among Rocks.* Although it reads in a few places like prose statements chopped up to fit arbitrary line lengths, for the most part this new, plain, direct style, reinforced with controlled repetition of word and image, is a suitable vehicle for focussing attention not on itself but on key political events and the counterpointed themes of love and violence.

As with topical poetry in general, certain of the references in "Nocturne" and other poems of *Theme and Variations for Sounding Brass* have already become clouded with time. The average reader probably does not remember that Anatoly Dobrynin ("Johnson listened to Dobrynin/impassively") was Soviet Ambassador to the United States during the Johnson administration, for example. Yet "Nocturne" is a powerful, unique, and important poem, significant in Gustafson's artistic evolution for its striking immediacy, objectivity, new proselike clarity, and political themes, as well as for its definition of love in an enlarged socio-political context. The poem ends:

> it comes home
> to my mind,
> the denial, even the intimacy of
> love, how,
> when Prague
> is silent.

2. *"Fantasia"*

A fantasia is normally a composition written quickly, the direct product of the composer's impulse. The term is also applied to works built on already existing musical themes. Both senses of the word are applicable to Gustafson's "Fantasia on Four Deaths," a poem about the tragic shooting of thirteen students—four fatally—by Ohio National Guardsmen on the campus of Kent State University, Kent, Ohio, on 4 May 1970. Begun a few weeks after the event, this poem was finished within a couple of days; the counterpointed themes of love and violence at the time already existed in the Gustafson canon, the most recent example being "Nocturne: Prague 1968."

Gusfafson's sources for "Fantasia" include *Life, Time,* the *New Yorker,* and the *New York Times.* The latter not only provided him with detailed reports about the Kent State tragedy, and later about investigations into the events, but it also printed on Sunday, 10 May, a collection of excerpts of comments about student radicals and other dissidents from the political speeches of then Vice President Spiro Agnew. These excerpted speeches contain inflammatory remarks about "tomentose exhibitionists," "an effete corps of impudent snobs who characterize themselves as intellectuals," as well as provocative statements such as "a snivelling, hand-wringing power structure deserves the violent rebellion it encourages. If my generation doesn't stop cringing, yours will inherit a lawless society where emotion and muscle replace reason."[14] The distortion of peace, law, and order both in word and deed by government forces seeking to suppress dissidents is the central political theme.

Again as in "Nocturne," there is a structural contrast between nature—the university hill—and artillery; the students are identified with the life forces of nature; this is especially true of Allison Krause, one of the four killed, who had reportedly put a flower into a guardsman's rifle the day before her death with the remark "flowers are better than bullets." This gesture links her with the anonymous youth photographed by journalists in Czechoslovakia in 1968 during the Russian invasion putting a carnation into the barrel of one of the bristling crowd of rifles pointing at him; Gustafson, while documenting events in Ohio, indeed makes crossreferences to Prague, Vietnam, and finally to "all/ Self-propagated violence."

The main technical innovation in this poem is the use of an eyewitness persona; this makes "Fantasia" at least initially, the most personal and immediate of Gustafson's *engagé* poems. The opening reads:

> Four *impudent snobs*
> Fall. I was standing beside
> One, blood on her blouse
> (Prague on her blouse,
> Vietnam on her blouse).

The device partially breaks down at times, however, and there is a sense of incomplete identification in lines such as "Most likely/ There was silence" or "She's supposed to have said." Also, using a participant persona identified with the students, who nonetheless attempts to be as impartial as possible, leads to prosaic compromises:

> You can't expect blanks
> All the time. The Guardsmen
> Were tired. They undergo
> Relatively little discipline.

Elsewhere the assessment of apparently motiveless violence is quiet and convincing, however:

> There was silence, the instinctive hush
> Preceding the gentle press of
> Flesh on trigger
> Prolonged into fact though no one
> Knows whose is the motive
> Nor where it is pointed nor even
> The direction it is coming from. . . .

The recording of a topical military and political event, the basic contrast between peace and war or nature and artillery, the inclusion of excerpts from political speeches, and the ending in the persona's home environment—"this lake,/This territory green and lovely"—all recall "Nocturne." But the conclusion the persona reaches in "Fantasia" marks a step nearer to despair. The Quebec bird song finally is "mordent"—a musical pun on the keynote "mordant" with its etymological incorporation of death. Gustafson records this time not just denial of love, but indeed the threat of a pervasive and complacent loss of humanity.

3. *"Ricercare"*

The musical form of ricercare is an improvised ornamentation or variation whose origins are found in the Renaissance custom of transferring vocal polyphony to instruments. Gustafson's task in "Ricercare: And Still These Deaths Are Ours" (a poem commissioned by the C.B.C. to accompany pictures taken by Donald McCullin for the cover story of the *London Sunday Times Magazine* on 5 September 1971 entitled "And Still They Run: The Unabated Misery of West Bengal") involves a crossing over from one medium to another. Then, too, his treatment of death and love provides a variation on a recurring theme in his own writing, with numerous other literary connections as well (for instance, to Dylan Thomas's poem "A Refusal to Mourn the Death, by Fire, of a Child in London" which is cited in the final lines).

The central issue is the correct relation of the individual to society. This is underscored by the opening allusion to *Twelfth Night.* Sir Toby: "Dost thou think, because thou art virtuous, there shall be no more cakes and ale?" Clown: "Yes, by Saint Anne, and ginger shall be hot i' th' mouth too" (II, iii, 105-08). The Gustafson persona wonders out loud if he must "abolish pleasure" and practise "abstinence in bed" because of the tragedy in Bangladesh, and whether he has any individual obligation to become involved in the South-Asian disaster (figuratively, whether "I must pack my bag for Bangladesh").

Reviewing the ugly scenes of hunger, disease, misery, death, and futile if valiant attempts to nurture doomed love ones (such as the "Bengali Romeo" who carries his dying wife in his arms for miles along the muddy refugee trail), the persona acknowledges an urgent need for physical assistance—"Adequate medical/Supplies can do it. Clean hospitals"—but spiritual support is called for as well.

> I am thinking of compassion; clichés;
> Brotherly love; running politics
> And votes on compassion. A cliché, all
> Right—that idea, of scrubbing
> Man's dubious attentions to man
> With a vote, meeting cholera with love,
> That copulative pair with remembrance.
> . . . .
> The world is such
> That all we can do is send our love.

There seems to be finally no other solution but love, generalized into the political conception of compassion called for in the epigraph by Justice Earl Warren. Love remains Gustafson's only answer, no longer simply love on an individual level—as between mother and child, or husband and wife—but on a global, socio-political scale.

"Ricercare" is hortatory, didactic, and no doubt would be much improved in *Theme and Variations for Sounding Brass* were it accompanied by the visuals for which it was originally designed. But its humane cry for compassion to replace indifference, complacency, or numbness is wringing; its sensitivity and affirmation, compelling: "With all that dead to be occupied/With, they are still interested in living."

4. *"Aubade"*

An aubade is usually a light, cheerful piece of music; the name is derived from *"aube,"* the French word for dawn. Gustafson's "Aubade: Quebec" is thus ostensibly a counterpart to "Nocturne: Prague 1968." But as its byline indicates—"Laporte murdered, Autumn 1970"—ironically this dawn music ushers in a bleak time of terrorism and political murder. Originally entitled "Rhapsody on Two Dead: Cross and Laporte Murdered in Quebec, Autumn 1970," the poem was begun on 18 October, just after the institution by Prime Minister Pierre Trudeau of the emergency War Measures Act and a mistaken report of the death not only of Quebec Cabinet Minister Pierre Laporte but also British diplomat James Cross, both kidnapped by members of the Front de Liberation du Québec in 1970 (Cross alone being rescued alive).

Gustafson's sources, apart from his being physically in the penumbra, include *Time, Life,* the *Montreal Star,* and a booklet entitled, *The FLQ: Seven Years of Terrorism: A Special Report by*

the Montreal Star.[15] Knowledge of these secondary sources is
necessary to comprehend fully the topical allusions in this poem
which, like Yeats's "Easter 1916," is an extremely significant poem in
its national context, one which documents a radical and seemingly
irreversible social shift. The poem, narrated in fourteen staccato free
verse paragraphs, describes the cumulative terrorism in Quebec
which culminated in death and the shattering of Canada's faith in her
immunity to violent political struggle. Gustafson's first stanza
succinctly presents "All that was not possible/In a bloody trunk"—
the corpse of the murdered Laporte. As in "Nocturne," Gustafson's documentation is accurate here, even down to the licence
plate number on the death car abandoned in suburban Saint
Hubert.

The villains in Gustafson's "Aubade" are F. L. Q. terrorists and
sympathizers, including intellectuals Charles Gagnon, a Université
de Montréal sociologist who demonstrated in front of the United
Nations on behalf of the F. L. Q. and was eventually deported in
connection with the terrorist bombing of La Grenade Shoe Factory
in Montreal in 1966, and Pierre Vallières, author of *Nègres blancs,*
who was sentenced to life for manslaughter in this same incident (a
sentence on appeal reduced to thirty months). The poem's heroes are
the *chansonniers* who sing about love and the victims who have
forfeited life or limb. In a devastating parody of Elizabeth Barrett
Browning's "How Do I Love Thee?" in stanza eight, Gustafson rivets
attention on some of the victims: Wilfred O'Neill, the F. L. Q.'s first
victim, a nightwatchman killed in an explosion of a bomb planted
among garbage cans at a downtown Montreal recruiting center;
Sergeant Major Walter Leja, a demolition expert who dismantled
two Westmount mailbox bombs but was maimed for life when a third
exploded in his hands; Leslie MacWilliams, the store manager of the
International Firearms Company who resisted a raid by a five-man
gang and was shot dead; Thérèse Morin, an employee at a strike torn
Montreal shoe factory killed in the 1966 bomb explosion referred to
above; and Jeanne d'Arc St. Germain, a communications supervisor
killed when an early morning blast ripped through the National
Defence Communications Center in downtown Ottawa, the seventh
F. L. Q. victim in seven years.

The poem concludes with a terse rehearsal of the natural course of
life, which throws into relief the personal significance of these violent,
premature deaths and sets current Quebec events in the context of
universal truths.

A is not B
Nor death love.
We thought to sit in reason,
Truth among us.
We thought to have compassion,
Each man
His brevity, each his heritage,
His grief
And love.

As the leaf, yellow,
Strikes against the double glass,
This winter window,
So, man
His splendid season,
His certain life.

There is no retreat to a tranquil, restorative, springtime home
available now; violence, like winter, seems to blanket the whole
world, "The world in hostage to its arrogance."

5. *"Coda"*

When all variations are over, a coda adds a passage of sufficient
importance to represent the conclusion of the whole set instead of any
one of the separate component parts. Gustafson's "Coda: I Think of
All Soft Limbs," with its inclusive title, is intended as a summation
poem. It was begun on 9 November 1969, two days before the annual
international observance of Armistice, and was worked on until
January 1970 as political atrocities from Quebec to Biafra mounted.
In an unpublished preface to the poem, Gustafson noted that "it
seemed we were back in the 1930s. The mood of depression of all
intelligent men was the same as the mood I had presented in a poem
'April Eclogue' just before the Nazis marched into Poland, and in
the shorter poem 'Final Spring.'"[16]

In providing the conclusion for *Theme and Variations for
Sounding Brass,* this poem draws compassionate attention to victims
around the world: victims of political beatings under the military
dictatorship of Greek President Papadopoulos, the hundreds of
South Vietnamese victims found some nineteen months after the Tet
offensive of 1968 unburied in a creek bed and in shallow mass graves;
the hundreds of thousands of Bangladesh refugee children starving to

death in India; the thousands who were killed or died of starvation
during Biafra's secessionist struggle; Russian dissidents—including
writers Andrei Sinyavsky, author of *On Socialist Realism,* and Yuli
Daniel, outspoken short story writer, who were forced to stand trial
charged with disseminating slanderous material besmirching the
Soviet state and sentenced to seven and five years at hard labor
respectively, as well as Nobel Prize winner Alexander Solzhenitsyn
who was eventually exiled; protesting S. D. S. students (Students for
a Democratic Society) at Columbia University in New York ousted
from occupied buildings by police who axed down doors and
brutalized the students in the name of law and order; Jan Palach, the
Czech youth who immolated himself in defiance of the Russian
invasion; the Black American, Bill Terry, whose body was excluded
from Elmwood White Cemetery in Alabama; and Viet Cong
brutalized by American G.I.'s. In terms of both subject matter and
technique, Gustafson has done an about face from the introverted
Romanticism of his earliest verses; yet ironically the possibility
still exists here, as in all *engagé* literature, that even monstrous
international events and current public symbols will in time become somewhat obscure allusions. But perhaps this also serves
to underscore Gustafson's message: "The trouble is there is too/
Much death for compassion." Yet the quoted last word names
what he cherishes as the only possible solution to the world's
ills.

Theme and Variations for Sounding Brass as a whole is an
orchestrated study of violence; in it Gustafson deals with the ugliness
of war, torture, ignorance, poverty, starvation, political treason,
and murder; but, not stopping with the discovery that the world
is a terrible place, he avoids the charge which he levies in his criticism against the New Wave poets—that they are left in a negative position, failing to make clear what they would substitute
for the conventional values which no longer work.[17] His poems
pass from a realization of horror and failure to an affirmation
of charity, of the need for love and compassion, not only in individual but in social terms. Each of the five poems in this collection works towards its own statement or modification of this
basic position. The extraordinary affirmation of loving this imperfect and distorted world provides a remarkable example of
Gustafson's complex, trenchant, and humane insight into twentieth-
century civilization's alienation, moral degradation, violence, and
pervasive angst.

III   Fire on Stone

Named by Betty Gustafson during "that hour at Chartres Cathedral,"[18] *Fire on Stone* (1974)—radically different from *Theme and Variations for Sounding Brass*—celebrates individual moments of beauty and personal happiness, fleeting as they may be. "To hate mankind is but to judge Achilles only by his heel," Ralph Gustafson once noted,[19] and *Fire on Stone* in several ways provides an important counterbalance to the collection which immediately precedes it. While the poems of *Theme and Variations for Sounding Brass* testify to Gustafson's mastery of the public poem, *Fire on Stone* marks a sharp return to a more personal and reflective lyric mode as Gustafson resumes his study of nature, his world travels, and his Pound-like journey through the past to find touchstones which may still have relevance for citizens of the contemporary, polluted, war torn world.

Fire on Stone marks a high point in Gustafson's career: it is the first book to earn for him at last widespread critical acclaim in his own country. (Gustafson once commented sardonically: "I have been kept in the waiting room so long that I am almost weary of destination. My mature poetry is the product of heroism."[20]) Intellectual lucidity combined with passionate intensity and technical litheness makes this the work of a master. In poetry which is both compellingly direct and richly allusive, Gustafson studies the human condition in the context of this botched civilization, expressing a vision not just critical but also humane and consciously affirmative. Writing of the great composers ("Beethoven, Brahms & Co.") buried in the Central Cemetery in Vienna, Gustafson suggests that their compositions take note of

> various importances
> Such as major resolutions,
> Great scopes and heart-leaps
> While missing nothing humanly minor.[21]

Following *Theme and Variations for Sounding Brass* with its dissection of major public events, *Fire on Stone* with its celebration of private realities demonstrates Gustafson's similarly inclusive range and commanding virtuosity.

The collection opens with poems which set the context and give a critical assessment of the state of the world. "North Cape," the first

poem, juxtaposes natural beauty—"midnight sun," "fjord," "gulls"—
with manmade ugliness—"rubbish," "napalm." A fundamental opposition is suggested too between the persona and his lover on one
hand, and the engulfing natural and political environments on the
other. As Don Gutteridge noted in a review for *Queen's Quarterly,*
"everywhere the opposites grind together on the sensibility of one
with a keen eye and deliberate ear: domestic love is dwarfed by
Arctic landscape and tropical war."[22] Characteristic of Ralph Gustafson, reality is depicted as a play of dualities.

"Sunday Morning at Hammerfest," the second poem, is a companion piece. Originally titled "Sunday Morning of an Ex-
Christian,"[23] it articulates Gustafson's continuing quarrel with
the Christian emphasis on the symbol of the hanged Christ ("the
bloody/palms and feet/of overstretched Christ"). While not oblivious to death, pollution, and war, the persona chooses not to
renounce but to enjoy the world. Picking up the imagery of gull
and rubbish from "North Cape," the poem concludes in deliberate
affirmation:

> as
> for that gull
> there, now
> airborne over
> floating rubbish;
> the miracle of flight. (14)

By its very title, this poem invites comparison with Wallace Stevens's
"Sunday Morning," and it similarly rejects the Christian emphasis on
sacrifice, celebrating instead the sensuous beauty of the perishable
universe. Gustafson's final image, too, like Stevens's, is of a bird on
the wing.

In several more poems, Gustafson underscores his vision of the
world as an amalgam of stone and fire, debris and miracle, mud and
lotus. "Nails at Nijo" is a study in contrasts: order, goodness, and
beauty (symbolized by Michaelangelo's *Pieta* in Saint Peter's Basilica
in Rome), and their opposites (graphically represented in Lazlo
Toth's recent attack on this art treasure with a twelve-pound ham-
mer). "O Permanent Paean Periclean" is a strongly ironic song of
triumph about the human capacity for senseless destruction. Here
Gustafson draws attention to a classical example of architectural
harmony, beauty, and proportion: "The Parthenon. Men with their

damned/Wars blew it up." Noticing the defacement of Byzantine murals at Daphni, Greece, he generalizes:

> People aren't worth the world.
> Consider 'P. Kelly' cut
> In the mural paint of eleventh century
> Mary and her Jesus-child. (18)

A fuller history of the decline of civilization is given in "The Grandeur Was When." Tracing technological progress from the invention of the wheel to the discovery of the laser beam, the poem paints a bleakly humorous portrait of the modern, purified, sanitized, traffic jammed city and of greedy, aggressive urbanites who have a Pyrrhic love/hate relationship with nature.

> A thousand sluices play. In cities, purified
> Fountains please the air. Unto the moveable
> Hills his profits assigned, unamused,
> His love his own, by traffic processional to sanitized
> Valleys takes his turn, damned nature beaten. (27)

This poem is a linear descendent of the satirical "City Song" of *Flight into Darkness* and "On the Top of Milan Cathedral" of *Sift in an Hourglass*. A self-styled moral revolutionary who believes firmly in the social responsibility of the artist, outraged and discouraged by violence and pollution—"Phosphates," "Dead fish," "Pop bottles and fliptop/Cans"—Gustafson remains convinced that "The Thing to Do Is to Write More Poems" (28). He reasons in "Let Us Assert Affirmatives" that the horror of the decimation of Guernica has been made to shock the hearts of men and women around the world by Picasso's painting, and again that the repressive nature of the U. S. S. R. is repudiated in the defection of one of its leading ballerinas, Natalia Makarova. Individual achievements by artists and others thus remain possible.

Gustafson's antithetic view of reality and his unusually positive informing vision are given perhaps their most complete expression in "O Mud, Thou Vile Sublime." In lines which combine Elizabethan word play with contemporary conversational rhythms, Gustafson deliberately confounds categories. His persona asks with playful seriousness: "But what is grave? and quick? Life/Itself's a low-down buried pun." Mortality is inescapable; yet the poem affirms:

> Something's
> True amid all this slither surely?
> Tuesday wasn't it, we felt good?
> Heard caloo on back fences
> Dent this music with his mordents,
> Cock-crow surely dawn; this pulled
> And washed-out line of intimate Monday,
> A stretch of purest meanwhile briefs? (59)

The pun on "briefs" and the almost parenthetical placing of "meanwhile"—a word choice which itself underscores the temporariness of life—give this last line tragicomic possibilities; but the dominant note of the passage is celebration, for the satisfaction of Monday's wash or for Tuesday's treasured happiness.

Again in "To Old Asclepius—Lyric at Epidaurus," life is documented as being both painful and beautiful. Both are real—"Sting of wasp and swallow of moon." Ultimately, "The moment-when is what pertains" (58). This poem seems intended as a final statement. In a manuscript draft it is titled "Summation at Epidaurus," and the conclusion Gustafson reaches here is reiterated in many other places. Repeatedly he celebrates momentary joy: "An hour's magnificence" (68), "the flashed/Instant" (66), "Affirmation for the moment" (60). Gustafson's "moment-when" is comparable to Browning's infinite moment, Hopkins's inscape, Joyce's epiphany, or Lawrence's living moment. In fact, Gustafson once prefaced a reading of his own poems in 1972 at the University of Hawaii with this quotation from D. H. Lawrence: "The business of art is to reveal the relation between man and his circumambient universe, at the living moment."[24] His poetry urgently recommends that life be lived fully day by day, moment by moment. In the autumnal poem "Free Will Grabbed Back Again," Gustafson writes of "this day": "By Heaven! Live it and that/Is one more from the total/Damned mathematics" (33).

Unlike most contemporary Canadian writers, Gustafson in a theoretical universal tally seems to find that joy balances grief. "Landscape with Salmon Roses" openly suggests that "the roses/ . . . exact equality with grief" (67). In "Love Poem," characteristic of his poetry since *Sift in an Hourglass,* the lover-persona directly counterpoints the living and the dead; he sees that the skeleton's "grin's planted every/Time I look at my love" (32). "I reply: gayety [*sic*]" was the original final line, now deleted. It would have served only to underline what is already apparent in any case: that Gustafson's vision, like Yeats's, culminates in tragic gaiety.

"A Pile of Grave-Slates," inspired by a visit to the village church in East Coker, Somerset, where Eliot is buried, a poem resonant with echoes of traditional elegies including Gray's, is also unsettlingly jocular. Reminding us that "Death is for all," the ruin visiting persona winds to his conclusion with a citation from "East Coker": "There is no elegy. In my beginning/ Is my end./ Ha" (30). The ultimate note strikes grief and joy together. Similarly "Of Tigers and Pebbles," a poem about young children, concludes in unresolved paradox, tragically gay: "Oh I laugh with grief!" (29). His frequent paradoxes, puns, ironies, ambiguities, and poetic collages—piecing together disparate styles—all contribute to what Sandler has praised as "the perfect formal expression of double vision."[25]

Like "A Pile of Grave-Slates," "This Hospital Day Turns to Her," and several other poems, "Hyacinths with Brevity" impressively demonstrates Gustafson's technique of weaving together various styles—a technique first tried out in *Alfred the Great* and *Flight into Darkness* with strained and awkward results but now perfected—a technique, too, which owes much to his deep love for and knowledge of music. Since "the crabbed progression" from birth to death is already under way, planting bulbs which will not flower for many months constitutes an act of faith on the part of the persona and his wife. Life, death, beauty, love, ephemerality—the themes of this poem which turns on the metaphor of gardening all lie at the heart of Gustafson's work.

> You will use whatever watering can
> You can, what knife to plant the bulbs.
> I smell leaves and crab-apples
> On the ground; the crabbed progression is under
> Way, blossom poured, jelly
> In jars crimson in the sun along
> The sill. That hardens it, you tell me.
> I shall have toast in the morning.
>   But be quick.
> The valves of the heart are pesky things
> And shut down. We shall no more see
> The like of these leaves again. They blow
> Across the garden with this brief wind
> That blows. So you will use what you can.
> This trowel with last summer's caked
> Dirt on the blade, and this can
> And these forty bulbs which should be
> Already in the ground so swift the wind
> Blows and brief the constituency
> Of sun. This piece of hose will do . . .
> But you have the watering can. . . . (37)

"Hyacinths with Brevity," though inspired by homely, domestic routines, gently alludes to a wide spectrum of English literature from *Hamlet* to *The Waste Land.* Borrowing from tradition such expressions as "We shall no more see / The like" tends to reinforce the theme of transience on the level of style. Robin Skelton observes that Gustafson generally writes "in lines of verse whose thrust and counter-thrust, whose broken urgencies and sudden assertive rhetorics express the passionate ambivalence of the poems' message,"[26] his structures thereby fusing skillfully with his feelings about the interrelatedness of life and death. Characteristically, and clearly showing the influence of his musical background, Gustafson presents his experiences in counterpoint.

In another poem ostensibly about planting bulbs, "Poem in April," an Easter motif brings life and death into focus simultaneously as the gardener-persona plunges his hands into the earth and muses that "In a sense you could say / Christ smudged / My palm" (53). All living things are sacrificed to death, but out of death comes new life. Both "Hyacinths with Brevity" and "Poem in April," then, have strong connections with "Aspects of Some Forsythia Branches" of *Sift in an Hourglass* (in fact "Poem in April" was begun back in the mid 1960's). Confrontation with the realities of dissolution typically moves the Gustafson persona to affirm the renewal of life, "the wild / Paroxysm of the broken bud" (40).

Structural counterpoint is very much in evidence again in the two-part "Bishop Erik Grave's Grave." Built on two symbols, skull and sun, this poem is short enough to quote in full.

> Bishop Erik Grave's grave
> In the Aarhus domkirke
> Has a skull
> To show things up.
> Half a skull, really,
> The chaps fallen off,
> But still a skull.
>
> The sun's come out
> (It's been raining all day,
> On and off).
> The sun is out.
> Deny it who will. (89)

Images of sun, fire, and light recur throughout the collection as symbols of life and antitheses of stone, death.

Gustafson ties his affirmative vision to Wallace Stevens's whose influence on his poetry of the 1970's is considerable. "Wallace Stevens calls poetry a sacrament of praise. And if you don't praise life then . . . why write? Ultimately you've got to. And some of the latest poems say that OK we all suffer, but you remember your first ecstasy at least, or that flower's lovely, and you can't deny it. And if you deny it then you're the romantic, not me. You get that inverted romanticism which is so prevalent in contemporary Canadian poetry. And they think they're being realist when they write about bullshit, when in a sense they're being very romantic."[27]

In the end, of course, man is powerless against time and tide. King Canute, the subject of another fine meditation on death, showed his courtiers this after they flattered him there was nothing he could not do: he brought them all down to the seashore and then commanded the tide to come no further. Gustafson's "I Have Seen More of Canute Than He Did" continues:

> Time's tide goes on—with nothing
> More than a wash of saltfoam, weed
> And sandbug left, 1035
> Or now. (31)

Still, Gustafson's last words in *Fire on Stone* are resolutely triumphant. Typically, "Skull calls out the dancing bones."[28] The final poem is "The Star-Catcher" which ends: "battered / By burdens, he stands" (90). The human individual is a survivor, the "Nabob of bones" of the epigraph taken from Stevens's "Landscape with Boat." Like his mentor, Gustafson moves beyond a recording of the defects of the world and the mortal human condition to register his love of hoarded moments of joy, beauty, love, and devotion. That this process is illogical is irrelevant. From the time of *Rivers among Rocks* Gustafson had censured the "fool of intellect." In *Fire on Stone* he again stresses the irrational side of life, pointing out that "No man endures by reason / Alone and thought—foolishness that need not / Be said." "To Give Intuition a Certitude," from which these lines are drawn, urges most eloquently "That the desire / Be without reason; that the logic be love" (55).

Learned, intellectual, passionate, and pagan ("God is all things" [22]), Gustafson's poetry combines contradictions as he steers between Yeats's frenzy and Thomas's rage. His poems do not deny the incontrovertible and heart-rending facts of aging and death. "Less and less, I smell / Musk, I smell musk" (33), he records his lamentation for brevity with poignant simplicity. But despite these realities, Ralph Gustafson—to be ranked with Irving Layton and Leonard Cohen amongst Canadian love poets—writes with undaunted vitality and dignity out of the almost heroic conviction that "love supercedes all the tragedies of history,"[29] that "if you love, you will shake/Down with compassion the fixed immutable stars" (62).

IV Corners in the Glass

The motif of light again is an important strand in the intricately plaited imagery of *Corners in the Glass* (1977). As the sun, it symbolizes the life force; as reflected light, it suggests philosophical illumination—Joyce's *claritas*. The imagery, title, and epigraph from Stevens all indicate strong links between this work and its immediate predecessor. As one of the new poems explains, "World Increases with Thought of It," and this book, like *Fire on Stone,* is a sustained and impassioned meditation on existence. Shunning wholly abstract thought and pure speculation, Gustafson's intellectual grappling with the meaning of life issues here too in celebration of the tangible, audible, visible universe.

The title image recurs in the central part of Gustafson's "Argument," one of a series of three disputatious philosophical poems which provide the rational backbone of the book. "Argument," "Partial Argument," and "Further Argument" express Gustafson's maturing vision and articulate his ever deepening stress on the here and now. The movement away from religious, otherworldly solutions to the problems of the human condition, begun in *Flight into Darkness* and developed more fully in *Rivers among Rocks* and *Sift in an Hourglass,* is carried to conclusion in *Corners in the Glass* in readily accessible symbols or images and in pithy, direct language—a style which itself illustrates the primary thesis: "I'll have the concrete." Gustafson's "Argument" continues:

> Light, Erigina's Light
> (Capital L)'s
> An abstract absolute.
> I'll have sun
> On cranky crystal, corners in
> The glass, tablecloths and silver,
> Oranges with peels on them.[30]

The symbolism of light is universal, but in this poem Gustafson gives it a specifically Christian connotation by referring to the medieval church father, and of course repeatedly in the New Testament (in Luke, John, Thessalonians, Ephesians) those who are sons of God are called sons of light. The Gustafson persona rejects the self-sacrificing, orthodox Christian path to salvation; instead he puts his faith in concrete objects as news of God, and, like the figure in "Anniversary" of *Fire on Stone,* symbolically worships the sun.

"Partial Argument"—partial not so much because it is incomplete as because it is the discourse of one biased in favor of the arts— extends discussion into realms of aesthetics and morals. Patently a mouthpiece for Gustafson himself, the persona notes that the arts search for truth as precisely as the sciences, and perhaps more reliably since they do not build from hypotheses but from primal experience: "Coming across real poetry, owls hoot,/ Potatoes break ground, and coffee smells" (41). Beyond this, they are also moral activities. Thus he offers a definition of poetry as "the truth/ Plus trouble"—the trouble of craft and of interpreting, not just recording, life. Ultimately Gustafson's vision, close to Auden's, hinges on love. For him, the overriding question of the artist is "Does Jack love/ Jill?" (37).

Love is presented as of prime importance again in "Further Argument." The golddigger persona here figuratively indicates the dimensions of the poetic claim Gustafson has staked out for himself. While acknowledging the realities of hostile forces both inanimate ("wind," "mountains," "glaciers") and human ("shoot-outs"), the persona still resolutely digs for the gold ore, physical love. He comments: "I pack blankets and outride rackets/ On mute saddles, gain on shoot-outs/ With clasped thighs" (73). But a startlingly pessimistic hint that love may not in the end be able to save the human race from self-destruction is contained in this final portion of the book's core argument. The last image is of clocks running down, and the persona admits "Mortality and winter win." These suggestions of failure and resignation, reminiscent of the bleak outlook of the depression collection *Flight into Darkness,* mark a departure from Gustafson's almost consistently affirmative work of more recent years. Such signs are undoubtedly a concomitant of the poet's slowly nearing the end of his own life.

Four topical poems in particular emphasize brutality, war, and commercialism. These are "The Newspaper," "Process," "Scherzo" (memorable for its image of one of the world's great natural beauties diseased by technology—"At 8 o'clock Niagara Falls/ Breaks out in colours" [64]), and "Mothy Monologue." The latter, the most ambitious, recalls *Theme and Variations for Sounding Brass* in its focus on the atrocities of war in Southeast Asia and the Middle East. But here, too, the new mood of detachment is discernible; the poem's refrain, "My heart goes out," is paradoxically both persuasive and futile, suggestive equally of empathy and death.

For the most part, however, *Corners in the Glass*, like *Fire on Stone*, dwells on treasured moments of beauty and happiness; it stresses above all love, art, and sensual delight. In "Detail at Altamira," for example, prehistoric rock paintings drawn by primitive artists are counterpointed against and outweighed by present beauty—"The moment's melody of birds" (51). "An Instant of Grosbeaks" similarly celebrates momentary ecstasy. The imagery shifts from winter to summer and from Canada to Barbados as the persona in his imagination follows the flight of the migratory birds. Capturing the inscape of the grosbeaks on the wing seems to him sufficient compensation for mortality, the approach of winter, or death, which seasonal migration calls to mind.

A third fine poem on the *carpe diem* theme is "The Moment Is Not Only Itself." Gustafson's familiar gardener-persona is presented in this poem raking autumn leaves while recalling Chopin's Prelude in E^b Major. The joy and beauty of this October day seem able, at least momentarily, to create a favorable equipoise of opposites and "make end/Of foliage, of summer, descendings, however/You finish it, not matter" (45). In Gustafson's poems of the 1970's and even earlier, the joy of the moment is of supreme importance and carries significance for the future in much the same way that for Thornton Wilder love provides what immortality there is on earth. Thinking of love, Gustafson's persona concludes that "What is real is what the heart/Has" (44).

As early as *Flight into Darkness* Gustafson had begun to stress the concrete and the here and now. "A Candle for Pasch" from *Rivers among Rocks* had concluded with this-world emphasis: "Joy here, least: if none" (poem 10). "Apologue" had underscored that "taken joy is all" (poem 15). The persona of "Parable" had met "lethal beauty with furious praise" (poem 15); this is the same conviction that the speaking voice of "The Overwhelming Green" in the 1977 collection expresses.

> The green was overwhelming,
> Verdant or, trembled
> Against the sky, the sky
> Light blue, a blue
> That deepened as the eye
> Held on. It would have been
> Deprivation not to have
> Taken on death to see this. (43)

Here, as in several other reflective nature poems, Gustafson concentrates on common details in the immediate environment—on "here-exactness" (40)—as of paramount value. Throughout the collection, Gustafson seeks to uncover what is really important. The issue is raised directly in "Prelude," the first of the suite entitled "Phases of the Present." Out of a blue sky, a yellow ash leaf falls into the persona's lap, and he affirms "Of course it's important" (57)—both for its inherent beauty and for the larger thoughts of life and death it conjures up. Nature, pure sensation, art, poetry, music, sex, love—whatever creates beauty and joy is cherished. But perhaps the chief source of happiness now is nature.

One recalls that the persona of "At Moraine Lake" in *Rocky Mountain Poems,* having discovered that myths "lie," turned instead to "The irrevocable decisions of the ants" (19). Now "Myth and the Mountains" a second time juxtaposes Canadian and Aegean landscapes and legends. In the relatively young land of Canada where one is confronted with "beginnings to be shaped," there are no ancient temples or accessible, anthropomorphic, indigenous gods. In the Yukon there is only "the distance of snow/Without legend." Death menaces, but affirmation is possible:

> The field of white of crests, a love,
> As of beginnings to be shaped, whole
> And strived for, and though deathed,
> Had. (32)

The majority of the poems of *Corners in the Glass* is set in rural Canada, mainly in the environs of Gustafson's own home in North Hatley, Quebec. Like Pissarro, once persuaded by Degas to paint cabbages (an anecdote referred to in "Cabbages and Pianos: Impromptu"), Gustafson focusses on everyday events and commonplace activities in the immediate environment. Both literally and metaphorically, the cultivation of his own garden is a source of inspiration. This is the case for some of the most memorable poems in the collection, including "In Dispraise of Great Happenings," "Of Green Steps and Laundry," and "Philosophy of Cutting Petunias." The first of these is pivotal and directs attention to the fact that Gustafson, sharply criticized for being a Grand Tour poet in the 1960's, has become increasingly in recent years a regional poet, the Canadian equivalent in some respects of Robert Frost. His gardener-persona is no untutored country bumpkin, of course, as his several references to Liszt's Villa d'Este or the Trojan War underscore; however, what concerns him above all is not speculation but sensation, not history but geography, not the foreign but the local— the realities of flowers, bird song, and even the antics of midges at the corner of his patio on a summer afternoon. Enjoying the physical and aesthetically pleasing details of his own backyard, he confesses that he is content to remain "Oblivious of Agamemnon and a thousand ships" (17).

"Of Green Steps and Laundry" similarly celebrates tranquil, unselfconscious moments in the local routines of day-to-day living: a man's hammering a silver nail in a crooked green step, a woman's hanging blue and white shirts and a patched quilt on a squeaky line, a bird's coming to an overhead bough. These small details are important; out of moments such as these life is strung. The persona concludes:

> neither
> She nor the man pounding the clear air
> Fixing the green step with another nail,
> Will be aware of the importance, twenty
> Years later thought of by him ·.
> Who drove nails and saw laundry,
> Who thought little of cardinals and clothespins
> And now loves life, loves life. (16)

The love of ordinary events expressed in this pellucid and melodic poem recalls the theme of "Agamemnon's Mask: Archeological Museum, Athens" of *Ixion's Wheel* in which the persona found as much importance in the routines of living, loving, praying, and dying of an anonymous Achaean as in the great Agememnon's story. As Gustafson suggests again in "Philosophy of Cutting Petunias," these seemingly usual and even trivial activities—whether hammering a nail, hanging laundry, or cutting petunias to save them from frost— provide adequate "Compensations for days given to large/Enter-prise" (19).

In these regional poems, Gustafson picks up a thread worked earlier into the poems of place of *Rivers among Rocks* and throughout *Rocky Mountain Poems.* The book is rich in depictions of local flora and fauna: poplars, maples, peonies, petunias, lilacs, daisies, redpolls, cardinals, orioles, grosbeaks, spiders, squirrels, and ants. As such, the book is a sharp contrast to the foreign explorations of *Sift in an Hourglass* and *Ixion's Wheel,* as well as to the broad political perspective of *Theme and Variations for Sounding Brass.* Now Gustafson's attention is riveted not on alien history, politics, or art, but rather on native landscape and living creatures. He is one with those Canadians he describes in "Airborne Thanksgiving" as holding "thanksgiving and snow in their pockets" (31).

The poems of *Corners in the Glass,* furthermore, are mainly set in Canada in wintertime; they explore the Canadian psyche, the context of northness, and the anagogic equivalent of winter, age. The opening poem, "Wednesday at North Hatley," one of the best reflective lyrics in the entire Gustafson canon, is illustrative of these intertwined motifs.

> It snows on this place
> And a gentleness obtains.
> The garden fills with white,
> Last summer's hedgerow
> Bears a burden and birds
> Are scarce. The grosbeak
> Fights for seeds, the squirrel
> Walks his slender wire.
> There is a victory;
> The heart endures, the house
> Achieves its warmth and where
> He needs to, man in woollen
> Mitts, in muffler, without
> A deathwish, northern, walks.
> Except he stop at drifts
> He cannot hear this snow,
> The wind has fallen, and where
> The lake awaits, the road
> Is his. Softly the snow
> Falls. Chance is against him.
> But softly the snow falls. (13)

The setting in winter suggests difficult times. The grosbeak "fights" for seeds; the squirrel's wire is "slender"; birds are "scarce"; and the lone walker finds "Chance . . . against him." To this extent, the northern landscape is associated with struggle and death; but what Gustafson stresses is not the harshness as much as the beauty and even the gentleness of the snow sculpted scene, drawing attention to the facts that "The wind has fallen," "softly the snow falls," "a gentleness obtains," and that there is "victory" for "The heart endures, the house/Achieves its warmth." This poem is characteristic of Gustafson's Canadian landscapes in his later years. His country is no longer either literally or figuratively the angular, incisive, overpowering terrain of the Rockies. He paints the land now as being not only severe but also gentle, not just lonely but equally beautiful. Diverging from Frye, Jones, and Atwood, Gustafson's vision highlights neither terror nor bare survival but rather the meeting of challenge with strength, grace, and acceptance of loneness and, ultimately, even of death. In a recent interview, Gustafson elaborated on some of "those loved/Contradictions peculiar to people/Of seasons" that he mentions in "Airborne Thanksgiving."

I write about Quebec winter scenes. Compton. A little village where I used to play with a boy friend. We used to hang on freight trains as they came through. . . . A mile or two from any habitation, and yet to me that symbolized Canada. Waiting for the train to come through, and those parallels of the tracks which went into the horizon, that I wanted to go down. That whole thing was a longing, a loneliness, and yet a great love of having the source of those emotions. . . .

Margaret Atwood writes about survival. I have no sense of that cliffhanging from the Eastern Townships. And in my poetry I almost unconsciously oppose the idea that all Canadians do is cliff hang. In the Eastern Townships the winters are severe, there are blizzards, and I've written about that, but also it's very beautiful. And the challenge isn't so severe as it would be freezing in the muskeg or in the Laurentian Shield. What you've got is a sense of challenge which requires a certain amount of fortitude if it's thirty below zero, as it often is, but also a gentleness. My memories of winter are of a snowfall rather than a blizzard. I suppose you subsume that and you express it in your poetry as your Canada.[31]

Gustafson's view now is more mellow than in his earlier writing; his stress is not on defiance but on individual affirmation in the face of hardship, suffering, and reminders of death such as migration, seasonal change, and storm.

Finally Canada becomes a microcosm and a metaphor for life: it contains both good and evil, joy and sorrow, birth and death. "The

World Comes Up Suddenly" provides the counterpart to "Wednesday at North Hatley." This poem is another depiction of landscape with falling snow; but it rejoins nature poems such as the earlier "At Takkakaw Falls" in its presentation of a rough, inhospitable universe under a blinding, stinging storm. The landscape, like life, is not dependable. In "The Exact Worth of Trusting Sunlight" Gustafson uses the sun again as symbol of the life force, writing:

> The sun is hot, the sofa
> By the window the place to be,
> One lid closed against it while
> You read so razzle-dazzle
> Is it. But don't depend on it.

For suddenly,

> The next
> (Moment) dark fell down,
> The page of poems of dazzle-razzle
> Done in, the sun gone in. (91)

Still the challenge is "beautiful," the contradictions "loved" (31). As Gary Geddes noted in a review in the *Globe and Mail*: "Like the explorers he celebrates—'Those who tried to get there./Those not afraid of their country'—he seems finally at ease in the strange dispensation which is Canada, writing to his own people."[32]

Some of the poems in *Corners in the Glass,* then, focus on contemporary social and political struggles and others—the majority—on local beauty. In still others, these dual and contradictory aspects of reality are brought together, accentuating Gustafson's irony riddled double vision. Poems which fall into this last category include "Diabelli Variations," "Of Beds and Manuscripts," "Ostinato," and "Poem in Late August." In the first of these, the persona—a spokesman for Gustafson himself—reflects on how art has transmogrified the world resulting in the beauties of Botticelli's canvasses, King James's prose, Pound's poetry, or Beethoven's music. But he is also reminded of the fates of these famous artists: to go deaf, to be declared insane, and, of course, inevitably, to die. The world, he concludes, is a conglomeration of antipodean realities: "Husks and blossoming, sun and mud./No help for it." Yet life's tragedies may be met with dignity and courage, as the resilient symbol of Beethoven's successively larger ear trumpets proclaims: "At Bonn, in a case,/ Ear-trumpets against the stars" (36).

The movement from a registering of decline and decay to reaffirmation is repeated in the equally finely crafted and moving "Of Beds and Manuscripts." Built on a structural contrast between destruction and creation, the poem indicates the harsh realities against which Gustafson's affirmations are made. The poem catalogues the catastrophes that have befallen works of art throughout history: Sophocles' manuscripts, the bust of Queen Tiye, Titian's canvasses, a basket case from Vietnam. These objects remind him that the process of living means being "unfinished and hurt." Still, he speaks in the thundering last lines of creativity and love, as well as of wretched limitation: "My love waters gardens so they grow./ My love, by herself. At half-past two" (46). Woman, the feminine principle, like the treasured works of art even in their ruined state, assures continuity if not transcendence. Again in "Of Cordwood and Carmen" it is woman, humming as the sun goes down, who symbolizes fulfillment and joy. Gestures such as hers lead Gustafson to conclude that even now "Life's/ Heroic" (72).

"Ostinato" brings together two major motifs in *Corners in the Glass*—northness and affirmation. The chromatic imagery paints a striking contrast between the processes of death and life. The white of the snow throws into relief the red of the birds: one is the color of winter, death, and, in the East, mourning; the other, the color of blood, the life force. The persona, oblivious neither of the harshness of the season nor of war in Asia, rejoices in "this moment centred on/ Itself, red polls and snow" (67) and their brief beauty which is equally real.

"Poem in Late August" similarly is built on a strong contrast between death and life; its two-part structure recalls "Bishop Erik Grave's Grave" from *Fire on Stone,* while its mood is again almost tragically gay.

> I open again
> The passage in my side
> With the pair of eyebrow tweezers
> I keep handy
> For just such a purpose
> When the white
> At the opening won't
> Drain as it should.

> And the double-headed blossoms
> Of the orange lilies
> Are over the length
> Of the garden strip,
> And the blackberry bush
> Almost ready heavy
> With berries black
> For picking. (74)

In this poem and indeed throughout most of the collection, the persona seems a kin of the old man who narrates the short story "The Tangles of Neaera's Hair": both respond deeply and fully to the flash of a wing or the call of a flower in bloom.

Brevity and death, in fact, assume significance only for lovers of life: this is the theme of "Improvisations on Lines of Somebody Else." (The fact that here Gustafson's inspiration comes from lines written by fellow Canadian poet George Johnston quietly underscores in another way the nationalist theme of the collection and the repatriation of Gustafson's style.) This is a compelling and stirring metaphysical love poem in which the persona listens for his wife's arrival, her opening of the garage door. He reflects that "Nothing much matters really . . . love/Not in it." He asks, "Who's aware/Of the anonymous flaw who's not in love?" The idea is not new: the poem cites not only lines by George Johnston but also an earlier Gustafson poem, "The Meaning" (poem 16) from *Rivers among Rocks*. In "The Meaning" Gustafson abstracted from his emotion, writing: "No sooner love than hell and heaven/Batter at the pagan sense." Now his metaphysical insight is expressed through concrete, personal terms—"In the turn of a pulley, if she/Work it, life and death begin" (48)—so that the poetic style, like his major theme, embraces carnal realities.

Despite its impassioned love poems, affirmative nature poems, and stoic—even gay—meditations on the cycles of generation and ruin, *Corners in the Glass* finally is less optimistic than *Fire on Stone*. In the last poems, the persona seems strangely acquiescent before a vision of not just personal but global doom (although his cry is couched in beautiful and exquisitely crafted lines such as the melodic lament "Ladies Lovely" in which the passing of beauty is symbolized by the downfall of historical women). The most poignant example of this shift, "The Concrete Shall Outlast Us"—an extension and redirection of his argument in "Faith Is a Concrete Object"—is a

complex, mature, and sobering poem about the potential disap-
pearance of the human race. This poem seems in some ways to
develop out of the satirical stream in Gustafson's corpus—from the
parodic "Psalm 23: Revised Version" of *Flight into Darkness,*
through "Contrary to the Grandeur of God" of *Rocky Mountain
Poems,* to "The Grandeur Was When" of *Fire on Stone.* But irony
and caustic criticism are absent, as if it is now too late for
chastisement. The opening lines, with submerged imagery of shipwreck, faintly echo Pratt's conclusion in his story of disaster *The
Titanic,* while the verbal structure containing the vision of water
lapping around "the last red rock in the last/Of the sun" also recalls
Birney's finish in "David," his tragic story of maturation. Man, the
polluter and destroyer, has vanished leaving on the face of the earth
only sordid reminders of his wanton passage. "Paper flaps/At the
gate. A tooth-broken comb in the dried/Mud." But despite the
persona's overwhelming disappointment with *homo sapiens,* something positive remains; "the earth's grace will be left," he foresees.
Thus the final image is of "the still burning sun" (76).

But *Corners in the Glass,* unlike virtually every other Gustafson
book, does not end triumphantly. In "The Ember," contrasts between
ash and flesh are used in a discussion of life's passage to death. The
persona, confined in a wintry house ("House-nails ungrip/In the
boards. Snow creaks"), nonetheless manages to stay warm in front of
a hissing fire, and, though shaken, he throws back a shot ember,
"Flesh quick to get rid of it,/Heart tentative" (22). This symbolic
victory, however temporary, is not repeated in the final poem.
"Under the Drums and Tramplings" concerns burial. Although he
would rather think of bed, love, and green grass, the persona's
thoughts revolve around burial plots, urns, and "quiet bones" (92)—
not the "dancing bones" of *Fire on Stone.* Thus *Corners in the Glass*
ranges in subject matter from sensation to reflection, and from love
and creativity to destruction and death. It paints an impressive
collective portrait of the Canadian personality conditioned by
current events and the mammoth land, while it also offers penetrating
insights into one unique man from North Hatley, the maturing and
now retired poet himself.

CHAPTER 7

Conclusion

R ALPH Gustafson's canon continues to grow, his vision to mature, and his style to evolve in subtle ways. Still, there is already the work of fifty years to assess, including volumes of selected poems and stories chosen and arranged by the author. This body of work, constituting an important and highly distinctive link in the chain of the Canadian literary tradition, deserves wider attention than it has generally received, both for its uniqueness of orientation and technique and also for its significant dual relationship to the national tradition: Gustafson's writing from the 1920's through the 1970's presents in miniature the pattern typical of the overall growth of literature in Canada, and it also manifests a central Canadian concern with the antagonism between civilization and the wilderness.

In reviewing Gustafson's development, this study has noted how the poetry of his first phase from the mid 1920's to the mid 1930's—represented by *The Golden Chalice* and *Alfred the Great* (both published in London)—shows the extent to which he initially shouldered a thoroughly colonial sense of indebtedness to "the Greats" of British tradition, including Spenser, Shakespeare, and the Romantics. Yet amid this derivative juvenilia, inspired largely by historical incidents or famous ruins in Britain and continental Europe, are implanted the embryonic forms of themes which grow increasingly important in his mature work: love, death, nature, and the opposition of the temper of the times to the full and free cultivation of the arts. Further, a few early poems, dealing with the rural Canadian scene and written in a discernibly different and less imitative style, prefigure the strong engagement with place which also becomes more and more significant in the poems of later years.

Gustafson's poetry from the mid 1930's to the mid 1940's, culminating in the retrospective collection *Flight into Darkness* (published in New York), marks a second discrete phase in his development. During this transitional phase, his poetry expands to encompass themes of disillusionment and existential uncertainty. His style shows signs of ambiguity as well, being characterized by experimentation with new techniques borrowed from Modernists such as Hopkins, Eliot, Auden, Spender, and MacNeice, and also typified by very imperfect amalgamations of older with newer literary modes. Explorations of the themes of love and nature—now undertaken in the wartime context of mechanization, urbanization, and full-scale destruction—are marked by more concrete and objective treatment. Depicting the new world of the depression era breakdown, the volume reveals a significantly increased social consciousness and provides an important link between the veiled political allegory of *Alfred the Great* and the overt socio-political protest poetry of *Theme and Variations for Sounding Brass* thirty years later.

In the immediate postwar years, Gustafson redirected his creative energies from poetry to prose fiction. His short stories—psychologically penetrating and manifesting a deep awareness of sexual desires and repressions—are studies in the trauma of conflict between man and woman, parent and child, artist and society. Set largely in the Quebec townships, these stories expose Canadian puritanism and philistinism. Although generally written from a bleaker, more pessimistic perspective and focussing on unfulfillment and failures of love and communication, the stories exhibit many of the same values as the poetry.

The third and most interesting phase of Gustafson's work effectively begins in 1960; it includes four poetry volumes published during the 1960's—*Rivers among Rocks, Rocky Mountain Poems, Sift in an Hourglass,* and *Ixion's Wheel*—and four more during the 1970's—*Selected Poems, Theme and Variations for Sounding Brass, Fire on Stone,* and *Corners in the Glass.* All of these have been published in Canada. They reflect both a distinctively Canadian consciousness of the precarious position of the human individual set against the mammoth landscape or the implacable march of global events, and also a cosmopolitan and highly cultured awareness of Western tradition at large. The divergent pulls of European history and Canadian geography exist in a state of mutual tension in Gustafson's writing and run parallel to conflicts in his personal life with its alternations between his birthplace and current home in rural Quebec on the one hand, and sophisticated foreign cities—Oxford, London, New York—on the other. For example, in his 1960's poetry alone, there is the highly "aboriginal" collection of Rocky Mountain nature poems recorded in stripped down lines, as well as the highly "original" two subsequent collections based on travel to distant parts of the world and written in a richly allusive style. Gustafson's two voices can be heard again in the 1970's poetry; but just as the more modern parts of his sensibility clearly dominate the traditional parts now, so too those poems which ring with an authentic spirit of place increasingly replace those which shine in the reflected light of foreign cultures and allegiances.

It is not possible to speak of a unidirectional repatriation of voice and vision; Gustafson's current mentors—Pound and Stevens—are American, and his very latest book, *Soviet Poems,* is the diary of a trip outside Canada (his invited reading tour of the Soviet Union in the fall of 1976). Yet this does not invalidate the judgment that the major emphasis in his poetry of the past decade considered as a whole is on Canadian experience—his own—as it is conditioned by this lonely, magnificent, northern land. In his recent writing, Gustafson demonstrates not the Thomas Wolfe wisdom that one can't go home again, but rather the truth of Margaret Laurence's diviners that one *must* go home again. In the life-long process of uncovering this truth in his own way, Ralph Gustafson has produced an impressive body of poetry which bears witness to a personal, as well as a national, struggle. This emphasis on place also links Gustafson with several other distinguished postcolonial writers, such as Derek Walcott, Wilson Harris, and Patrick White.

Still, his main themes remain universal; they include statements of the primacy of the life of the senses over the intellect, celebrations of love whether between individuals or in a larger socio-political context, delight in the beauties of nature and the quasireligious transcendence they evoke, protest against man's pollution and urbanization of the environment, and passionate defiance—even ultimately dignified acceptance—of both ephemerality and death.

Paralleling Gustafson's shifts in subject matter between the foreign and the local are his stylistic movements from obscurity to simplicity. Many of his poems resonate with literary, mythological, and historical allusions, making his work distinctive and highly learned. Yet the mellifluous sounds and exact rhythms which carry this weight stand among his most significant accomplishments. Despite his general reputation as an extremely difficult if expertly skilled craftsman, Gustafson has modified his style noticeably in recent years to make it more lucid and direct—in the mixed media protest poems of *Theme and Variations for Sounding Brass* almost prosaic, in fact.

Many of Gustafson's poems and stories are critical of the times and their tyranny of the unimaginative, but his dominant mood—almost wholly unique among his peers—is joyously affirmative. Particularly in *Fire on Stone,* he celebrates with passion the mystery and marvel of the universe grasped in isolated moments of insight—"the moment-when." In his later years, he writes with sharper regional focus—"here-exactness"—on precisely those luminous details which assess absolutes.

Conclusions as to the ultimate significance for world literature in English, or even the more circumscribed Canadian literary tradition, of the work of a writer still actively publishing, whose technique and outlook continue to evolve, must inevitably remain fluid. But it seems possible to indicate even now that Gustafson's work, which has been admired by a relatively small group so far, will in the future be assessed as belonging centrally to the mosaic of the Canadian experience. Gustafson's stylistic development is typical of the growth of poetry in general in Canada, while the struggles and competing loyalties which his writing structures stem from the same sources of conflict many other Canadian writers from Heavysege to Cohen have struggled to reconcile also. The tension between civilization and wilderness—a principal motif in Gustafson's work—is a major theme in Canadian literary tradition at large, as D. G. Jones has persuasively demonstrated. Gustafson's vision, while affirmative and even defiant, ultimately does fall under the terms of reference of Jones's sacrificial embrace and thus again is part of the mainstream national tradition.

Like many of his contemporaries, Gustafson is calling for a saner and more spiritual world; an end to the destruction of the environment; and a halt to political brutality, social injustice, and ignorance. But his orientation is uncharacteristically positive—and even in basic ways Romantic—having faith in the restorative potential of the contemplation and enjoyment of nature. Thus Gustafson offers a rare combination of the committed and reflective writer, of a man who values both the life of the senses and the heritage of the arts, of a person who is both nationalist and postnationalist. His style fuses intellect with passion, dignity with indignation, and refinement with simplicity, while his chief themes emphasize love, a broad generally operative humanism, and deep inexhaustible compassion. Linda Sandler with justice has hailed Gustafson as "one of the most complete Canadian poets"[1] for having a metaphysic, a wide cultural range, and an affirmative vision. Joe Rosenblatt repeats that

Gustafson has tried "to ambitiously span a wide area of human consciousness," and he concludes that "he has largely succeeded."[2]

Gustafson's final achievement, then, has been to embrace a broad spectrum of literary tradition and cultural reference while also, in a national context, breaking new ground. The equal and even the superior of more celebrated contemporaries A. J. M. Smith, Earle Birney, and Irving Layton, he has staked a valid and enduring claim among the foremost ranks of Canadian poets. Ultimately his unified but constantly evolving vision, combined with his impeccable and vital artistry, deserves to win Gustafson wide national and international acclaim as a postModern Canadian poet of the first order.

Notes and References

Chapter One

1. "Personal Statement," part of typescript "Additional for *Contemporary Poets*" in Gustafson's possession. Gustafson is included in *Contemporary Poets of the English Language,* ed. Rosalie Murphy (Chicago, 1970), pp. 456-57.

2. Correspondence: Yousuf Karsh to Wendy Keitner, 21 August 1972.

3. Interview by Linda Sandler, Toronto, 20 August 1975, transcript p. 3.

4. Ibid.

5. Gustafson is reluctant to discuss details of his personal life during these middle years in London and New York where he and Ellen Ballon resided in adjoining apartments on West 67th Street. Ballon is deceased. One can only speculate on the autobiographical origin of the early love poems and the failed affairs of lovers in numerous of Gustafson's short stories of the late 1940's and early 1950's.

6. Correspondence: Ralph Gustafson to Robert Finch, 7 November 1946, in Ralph Gustafson Literary Papers, Murray Memorial Library, University of Saskatchewan, Saskatoon (hereafter referred to as Gustafson Papers [Saskatoon]). Pelham Edgar reinforces this evaluation in a review of the anthology in "Canadian Poetry Reviews," *Canadian Poetry Magazine,* 6 (October 1942), 31. See also E. K. Brown, "Letters in Canada: 1942," *University of Toronto Quarterly,* 12 (April 1943), 311.

7. The idea for this joint anthology was proposed by A. J. M. Smith in a letter to Ralph Gustafson on 26 June 1941. By the following April, a manuscript had been prepared and submitted to King Gordon of Farrar and Rinehart. In correspondence of 11 June 1942 Smith writes: "The Chicago University Press are seriously interested in my big affair [*The Book of Canadian Poetry*] and I don't want to damage its chances by publishing another anthology before it comes out. I asked Gordon to mail the ms. back to me in Montreal, and I will incorporate a good part of it into my big book. I trust this is all right with you." Gustafson's reply is dated 11 July 1942 and like the earlier letters is in the Gustafson Papers (Saskatoon): "No, I didn't know King Gordon had sent the MS back. I feel sure I could find a publisher here other than F. & R." The dialogue breaks off here, and Smith's anthology does not mention any collaboration with Gustafson; Northrop Frye later

notes "a remarkable coincidence of taste between the two anthologists."
Correspondence: Northrop Frye to Wendy Keitner, 2 May 1973.

8. A second performance was given at the University of Cincinnati. Later
the ballet music was transcribed for solo orchestra and, now called
"Movements for Orchestra," won second prize at the Concorso Inter-
nazionale in Italy. It was eventually recorded on long-playing disc Stereo LS-
665 under the label "The Louisville Orchestra, First Edition Records."

9. Correspondence: Ralph Gustafson to Wendy Keitner, 1 December
1972.

10. Introduction, *Poets of the Confederation* (Toronto, New Canadian
Library, 1960; repr. 1969), p. xi.

11. At the time of writing, *Soviet Poems* is forthcoming from Turnstone
Press, University of Manitoba, Winnipeg.

12. For further discussion of this theme in Canadian literature see "The
Problem of Job" in D. G. Jones, *Butterfly on Rock* (Toronto, 1970), p. 87.

Chapter Two

1. (Harmondsworth, 1958; second rev. ed. 1975), p. 23. All future
references to this anthology will be to the in-print edition and will be included
in the text.

2. "Explanation," *The Golden Chalice* (London, 1935), p. 23. All future
references to this volume will be included in the text.

3. Unpublished Master's thesis, Bishop's University, Lennoxville, 1930,
p. 1.

4. (London, [1937]), p. 18. All future references to this play will be
included in the text.

5. Correspondence: Earle Birney to Ralph Gustafson, 5 April 1942,
Gustafson Papers (Saskatoon).

6. Correspondence: Ralph Gustafson to Earle Birney, 13 April 1942,
Gustafson Papers (Saskatoon).

7. Colonel Wilfred Bovey, "Radio Drama," *Saturday Night*, 53 (14 May
1938), 14.

Chapter Three

1. The MS of *Flight into Darkness*, including a handwritten list giving
the dates of composition of most of the poems, is among the Gustafson
Papers (Saskatoon) except for the MS of the section entitled "Sequence to
War" which is housed in the Lockwood Memorial Library at the State
University of New York at Buffalo.

2. *Flight into Darkness* (New York, 1944), p. 59. All citations of poetry in
Chapter 3 are to this collection rather than to the rare limited editions of the
individual booklets. In future references, page numbers are included in the
text.

3. "Canadian Poetry," *Canadian Forum*, 20 (August 1940), 155.

4. "Theme with Variations," review of *Flight into Darkness, The New Republic*, 2 April 1945, p. 453.

5. "Letters in Canada: 1941," *University of Toronto Quarterly*, 11 (April 1942), 290.

6. Review of *Flight into Darkness, First Statement*, 2 (February–March 1945), 32.

7. In New York during the war years, e. e. cummings once commended Gustafson as "one of the few modern poets who can write a love lyric." Correspondence: Ralph Gustafson to Wendy Keitner, 19 January 1978.

Chapter Four

1. *Dalhousie Review*, 32 (Summer 1952), 134.

2. *The Brazen Tower* (Tillsonburg, Ontario, 1974), p. 46. All future references to Gustafson's short stories will be to this collection unless otherwise indicated, and page numbers will be included in the text.

3. Margaret Atwood, *Survival* (Toronto, 1972), p. 208.

4. For a fuller discussion of the theme of victimization in Canadian literature see Atwood's outline of "Basic Victim Positions" in *Survival*, pp. 36–39.

5. *Second Image* (Don Mills, Ontario, 1971), p. 92.

6. *Queen's Quarterly*, 67 (Spring 1960), 47.

7. *Here and Now*, 1 (January 1949), 50. Future references to this story, which is not collected in *The Brazen Tower*, will be to this journal and will be included in the text.

8. *Tamarack Review*, 10 (Winter 1959), 14. Future references to this story will be to this journal and will be included in the text.

9. "No Music in the Nightingale: An Ironic Comedy," TS 9, 151. The typescript of this unpublished novel is in Ralph Gustafson's possession. Future references to the novel are to this typescript and are included in the text.

10. Atwood, *Survival*, p. 208.

10. Atwood, *Survival*, p. 208.

Chapter Five

1. At the time of this writing, *Soviet Poems* is in press.

2. "Am Bachsee, with Thoughts of Vietnam," *Ixion's Wheel* (Toronto, 1969), p. 109.

3. "Dr. Johnson Kicks Hocking's Shin," *Rivers among Rocks* (Toronto, 1960), poem 29. Poems, not pages, are numbered in this collection; future references to this volume are included in the text.

4. "Two Canadian Poets: Ralph Gustafson and Eli Mandel," *Culture*, 22 (June 1961), 147.

5. Interview with Linda Sandler, Toronto, 20 August 1975, transcript p. 10.

6. "Poetry to No One Else: Six Gestures of Lyric Response," *Queen's Quarterly,* 68 (Summer 1961), 347.

7. "Free Will Grabbed Back Again," *Fire on Stone* (Toronto, 1974), p. 33.

8. The MS of *Rivers among Rocks* is in the Ralph Gustafson Literary Papers at Queen's University, Kingston, Ontario (hereafter referred to as Gustafson Papers [Kingston]).

9. "Introduction," *Poets of Contemporary Canada 1960-1970,* ed. Eli Mandel (Toronto, 1972), p. xiii.

10. Michael Hornyansky, review of *Ixion's Wheel* in "Letters in Canada: 1969," *University of Toronto Quarterly,* 39 (July 1970), 328; and Ralph Gustafson, "At Moraine Lake," *Rocky Mountain Poems* (Vancouver, 1960), p. 18.

11. "Canada and Its Poetry," review of *The Book of Canadian Poetry* by A. J. M. Smith, *Canadian Forum,* 23 (December 1943), 207-10; repr. in Northrop Frye, *The Bush Garden: Essays on the Canadian Imagination* (Toronto, 1971), pp. 129-43.

12. *Contemporary Verse,* 1 (December 1941), 6.

13. *Fiddlehead,* No. 22 (November 1954), pp. 1-2.

14. Review of *Rivers among Rocks, Fiddlehead,* No. 48 (Spring 1961), p. 52.

15. Vernal House, "A Canadian Poet Comes into Focus," *Globe and Mail,* 4 February 1961, p. 16.

16. "At Moraine Lake" and "In the Yukon," *Rocky Mountain Poems* (Vancouver, 1960), pp. 18, 36. Future references to the poems of this volume (most of which are reprinted with minor revisions both in *Ixion's Wheel* and *Selected Poems*) will be to this original edition unless otherwise indicated and will be included in the text.

17. The MS of *Rocky Mountain Poems* is in the Gustafson Papers (Kingston).

18. Revised version of "Into the Tonquin Valley," *Ixion's Wheel,* p. 16.

19. *The Collected Poems of Wallace Stevens* (New York, 1954; repr. 1976), p. 512.

20. This frequently anthologized poem can be found in A. J. M. Smith, *Poems: New and Collected* (Toronto, 1967), pp. 50-51.

21. Revised version of "At Moraine Lake," *Ixion's Wheel,* p. 20.

22. Revised version of "On Mountain Summit," *Ixion's Wheel,* p. 32.

23. Correspondence: Ralph Gustafson to Wendy Keitner, 29 April 1973.

24. Revised version of "On the Columbia Icefield," *Ixion's Wheel,* p. 17.

25. "The Poem That Took the Place of a Mountain," *The Collected Poems of Wallace Stevens,* p. 512.

26. Revised version in *Ixion's Wheel,* p. 31.

27. "The Wreck of the Deutschland," *The Poems of Gerard Manley Hopkins,* eds. W. H. Gardner and N. H. MacKenzie (London, fourth ed. 1967), p. 52.

28. The MS of *Sift in an Hourglass* is in the Gustafson Papers (Kingston).

29. *Fiddlehead*, No. 70 (Winter 1967), p. 62.

30. *Sift in an Hourglass* (Toronto, 1966), p. 13.

31. *Butterfly on Rock*, p. 139.

32. Correspondence: Ralph Gustafson to Desmond Pacey, 7 January 1967, in Gustafson Papers (Kingston).

33. Unnumbered page of transcript of interview by Linda Sandler, Toronto, 20 August 1975.

34. "The Concrete Paradise: The Major Theme of Ralph Gustafson's *Fire on Stone*," *Fiddlehead*, No. 104 (Winter 1975), p. 110.

35. S. P. Zitner, *Canadian Forum*, 49 (March 1970), 299.

36. "Voices in the Dark," *Canadian Literature*, No. 45 (Summer 1970), p. 71.

37. Irving Layton, *The Whole Bloody Bird*. (*Obs, Aphs & Poems*) (Toronto, 1969), p. 139.

38. Correspondence: A. J. M. Smith to Ralph Gustafson, 2 November 1969, in Gustafson Papers (Kingston).

39. *Ixion's Wheel* (Toronto, 1969), p. 82.

40. "Less Than Meets the Eye," 9 May 1970, p. 4.

Chapter Six

1. Interview with Linda Sandler, Toronto, 20 August 1975, transcript p. 9.

2. Ibid.

3. "Temperament Versus Technique," review of *Fire on Stone, Canadian Literature*, No. 64 (Spring 1975), p. 112.

4. "A Tilting Equipoise," *Canadian Literature*, No. 58 (Autumn 1973), pp. 82–83.

5. "A Rare Sense of the Continuity of Things," review of *Selected Poems* and *Theme and Variations for Sounding Brass, Saturday Night*, 87 (December 1972), 56.

6. This statement is made in connection with the defiant philosophy of *Fire on Stone*. Notes for interview of Ralph Gustafson, unnumbered page of transcript.

7. "Carta Canadensis," *Selected Poems* (Toronto, 1972), p. 72.

8. "Canada in a Word," broadcast 23 February 1972, Australian Broadcasting Commission, Sydney: published in *New Mitre* (Lennoxville, Quebec, 1973), p. 9.

9. "Coda: I Think of All Soft Limbs," *Theme and Variations for Sounding Brass* (Sherbrooke, 1972), poem 5 (unpaged).

10. Interview by Linda Sandler, Toronto, 20 August 1975, transcript p. 24.

11. Correspondence: Richard Arnell to Ralph Gustafson, 15 May 1970, in Gustafson Papers (Kingston).

12. Doug Fetherling, "A Rare Sense of the Continuity of Things," *Saturday Night*, 87 (December 1972), 57. Correspondence: George Jonas to Ralph Gustafson, 4 August 1972, in Gustafson Papers (Kingston).

13. The MS of *Theme and Variations for Sounding Brass*, together with clippings from Gustafson's various news sources, is in the Gustafson Papers (Kingston). This documentation was augmented by Gustafson's own visit to Prague one year after the invasion.

14. *New York Times*, 10 May 1970, section 4, p. 3.

15. The latter is the most complete source of information: *The FLQ: Seven Years of Terrorism*. A Special Report by *The Montreal Star*. Text by James Stewart. Published by *The Montreal Star* in cooperation with Simon and Schuster of Canada Limited (Richmond Hill, Ontario, 1970).

16. "Preface to Commercial Tape CBC of 'I Think of All Soft Limbs,'" in the Gustafson Papers (Kingston).

17. "New Wave in Canadian Poetry," *Canadian Literature*, No. 32 (Spring 1967), pp. 6–14.

18. Dedication, *Fire on Stone* (Toronto, 1974).

19. "Towards a Noticeable Notebook," p. 1. In Gustafson's possession.

20. Ibid.

21. "Zentralfriedhof, Vienna," *Fire on Stone*, p. 80. Future references will be included in the text.

22. "Poetry," 82 (Spring 1975), 140.

23. The MS of *Fire on Stone* is in the Gustafson Papers (Kingston).

24. Typescript of "Poetry Reading: University of Hawaii, March 29, 1972," p. 2. In Gustafson's possession.

25. "Gustafson & Others," review of *Fire on Stone, Tamarack Review*, No. 64 (November 1974), p. 90.

26. "Ralph Gustafson: A Review and Retrospect," *Mosaic*, 8 (Winter 1975), 169.

27. Interview by Linda Sandler, Toronto, 20 August 1975, transcript p. 10.

28. The MS of *Fire on Stone* shows that this volume was originally entitled "The Dancing Bones" after the poem which now appears on p. 40. The quotation is the MS version of the last line of this poem; it has been deleted in the published version.

29. "Poetry Reading: University of Hawaii, March 29, 1972," p. 5.

30. *Corners in the Glass* (Toronto, 1977), p. 34. Future references will be included in the text.

31. Interview by Linda Sandler, Toronto, 20 August 1975, transcript pp. 3-4.

32. 7 January 1978, p. 37.

Chapter Seven

1. "Gustafson & Others," *Tamarack Review*, No. 64 (November 1974), p. 92.

2. "Filet Mignon Poetry," *Canadian Forum,* 54 (November–December 1974), 20.

Selected Bibliography

PRIMARY SOURCES

A. Books of Poetry

Alfred the Great. London: Michael Joseph, [1937].

Corners in the Glass. Toronto: McClelland and Stewart, 1977.

Epithalamium in Time of War. New York: privately printed by L. F. White, 1941.

Fire on Stone. Toronto: McClelland and Stewart, 1974.

Flight into Darkness. New York: Pantheon Books, 1944.

The Golden Chalice. London: Ivor Nicholson and Watson, 1935.

Ixion's Wheel. Toronto: McClelland and Stewart, 1969.

Lyrics Unromantic. New York: privately printed by L. F. White, 1942.

Poems (1940). Reprinted from *The Sewanee Review,* 48 (April–June 1940), 236–44.

Rivers among Rocks. Toronto: McClelland and Stewart, 1960.

Rocky Mountain Poems. Vancouver: Klanak Press, 1960.

Selected Poems. Toronto: McClelland and Stewart, 1972.

Sift in an Hourglass. Toronto: McClelland and Stewart, 1966.

Soviet Poems. Winnipeg: Turnstone Press, 1978.

Theme and Variations for Sounding Brass. Sherbrooke: privately printed by Progressive Publications, 1972.

B. Collected Short Stories

The Brazen Tower. Tillsonburg, Ontario: Roger Ascham Press, 1974. Contains the following stories: "Summer Storm," "The Human Fly," "Surrey Harvest," "The Circus," "The Pigeon," "The Paper-spike," "Heaven Help Us," "Shower of Gold," "The Tangles of Neaera's Hair."

C. Uncollected Short Stories

"Snow." *Queen's Quarterly,* 67 (Spring 1960), 47–53; *Journal of Canadian Studies,* 4 (Fall 1969), 3–6.

"The Thicket." *Cross-Section 1948: A Collection of New American Writing.* Ed. Edwin Seaver. New York: Simon and Schuster, 1948, pp. 334–41; *Here and Now,* 1 (January 1949), 48–52.

"The Vivid Air." *The Tamarack Review,* No. 10 (Winter 1959), pp. 8–19.

D. Editions

Anthology of Canadian Poetry (English). Harmondsworth, Middlesex, England: Penguin Books, 1942.

Canadian Accent: A Collection of Stories and Poems by Contemporary Writers from Canada. Harmondsworth, Middlesex, England: Penguin Books, 1944.

"Canadian Women Poets." *Voices*. Commonwealth Issue, No. 133 (Spring 1948), pp. 26–37.

A Little Anthology of Canadian Poets. Norfolk, Connecticut: New Directions, 1943.

The Penguin Book of Canadian Verse. Harmondsworth, Middlesex, England: Penguin Books, 1958; rev. ed. 1967; second rev. ed. 1975.

Poetry Pilot: The Bulletin of the Academy of American Poets. Canadian Issue (August 1961).

Voices. Canadian Issue, No. 113 (Spring 1943).

SECONDARY SOURCES

A. Articles and Sections of Books

BEATTIE, MUNRO. "Poetry (1935–1950)." *Literary History of Canada: Canadian Literature in English*. Gen. Ed. Carl F. Klinck. Toronto: University of Toronto Press, 1965; rev. 3 vol. ed. 1976; Vol. 2, pp. 294–96. Briefly outlines the three phases of Gustafson's poetic development from 1935 to 1960.

DUDEK, LOUIS. "Two Canadian Poets: Ralph Gustafson and Eli Mandel." *Culture*, 22 (June 1961), 145–51. An impressive pioneering study tracing a division in Gustafson's work between poetry of mythological abstruseness and apparent remoteness, and poetry of direct and immediate relation to concrete issues.

FETHERLING, DOUG. "A Rare Sense of the Continuity of Things." Review article on *Selected Poems* and *Theme and Variations for Sounding Brass*. *Saturday Night*, 87 (December 1972), 56–57. Focusses on the tug-of-war in Gustafson's poetry between modernity and tradition, with the modern self winning.

SKELTON, ROBIN. "Ralph Gustafson: A Review and Retrospect." Review article on *Fire on Stone*. *Mosaic*, 8 (Winter 1975), 167–79. The most penetrating and complete assessment of Gustafson's achievement published to date, underscoring Gustafson's range of interests, depth of learning, wit, and technical virtuosity.

B. Additional Reviews

LANE, TRAVIS. "The Concrete Paradise: The Major Theme of Ralph Gustafson's *Fire on Stone*." *The Fiddlehead*, No. 104 (Winter 1975), pp. 106–10. Focusses on Gustasfson's perception of the dual nature of reality—a combination of grief and joy—and notes his similarity to Wallace Stevens.

LILLARD, CHARLES. "Review." Review of *Selected Poems. Prism International,* 14 (Autumn 1974), 148–52. A personal statement about Gustafson's growing appeal and warm praise for him as a classical, humane, and cultured writer; ranks *Selected Poems* as one of the most powerful volumes of Canadian poetry published during the past twenty-five years.

MORSE, SAMUEL FRENCH. "Present Tense." Review of *Rocky Mountain Poems* and *Rivers among Rocks. Poetry (Chicago),* 98 (August 1961), 329–31. Comments on the split in Gustafson's poetry between language that attempts to be what it describes and language that simply describes, labelling him for *Rocky Mountain Poems* a poet of intense Canadian perception.

YATES, J. MICHAEL. Review of *Ixion's Wheel. Wascana Review,* 5 (August 1970), 105–07. Assesses the book as a fine balance between Gustafson's turning a classicist's eye towards primal Canada and turning a Canadian's eye towards the classical art and architecture of Europe and the Middle East; the most detailed of several reviews which focus on the split in this collection between wilderness and civilization.

C. Bibliography

ALLISON, L. M. and W. J. R. KEITNER. "Ralph Gustafson: A Bibliography in Progress, 1929–1972." *West Coast Review,* 9 (June 1974), 29–38. Needs updating, but is useful for its recording of Gustafson's periodical poetry and literary reviews, as well as for a fuller listing of secondary sources about Gustafson and his work.

Index